T0129421

S. A. MANOHARA

Unique Oneness Theory

Inquiry into the Confluence of
Psychology and Spirituality

BALBOA.
PRESS
A DIVISION OF HAY HOUSE

Balboa Press books may be ordered through booksellers or by contacting:

Balboa Press
A Division of Hay House
1663 Liberty Drive
Bloomington, IN 47403
www.balboapress.com
1 (877) 407-4847

Because of the dynamic nature of the Internet, any web addresses or links contained in this book may have changed since publication and may no longer be valid. The views expressed in this work are solely those of the author and do not necessarily reflect the views of the publisher, and the publisher hereby disclaims any responsibility for them.

The author of this book does not dispense medical advice or prescribe the use of any technique as a form of treatment for physical, emotional, or medical problems without the advice of a physician, either directly or indirectly. The intent of the author is only to offer information of a general nature to help you in your quest for emotional and spiritual well-being. In the event you use any of the information in this book for yourself, which is your constitutional right, the author and the publisher assume no responsibility for your actions.

Any people depicted in stock imagery provided by Getty Images are models, and such images are being used for illustrative purposes only.
Certain stock imagery © Getty Images.

Print information available on the last page.

ISBN: 978-1-5043-9783-4 (sc)
ISBN: 978-1-5043-9785-8 (hc)
ISBN: 978-1-5043-9784-1 (e)

Library of Congress Control Number: 2018901895

Balboa Press rev. date: 02/23/2018

Contents

Acknowledgments

Deepest gratitude to Shiromani Vijay, Renuka Kharkar, Arvind Vijayasarathi and Deepa Manohara for their enthusiasm and hard work and to all the friends and family whose contributions made this publication possible.

Foreword

I am truly honored to provide the foreword for Dr. S. A. Manohara's book, *Unique Oneness Theory*. I have known Dr. Manohara personally for over thirty years. We met in a psychiatric hospital, where we were both doing rounds after working in our own private practices. Dr. Manohara is a renowned and respected popular psychiatrist in our area of California, and I am proud to call him my friend.

Dr. Manohara's goal has been to meet all his patients' outpatient mental health needs at one convenient location and to ensure inpatient care when needed by creating a comprehensive mental health delivery system to care for the community. Today Truxtun Psychiatric Medical Group Inc. under his leadership has grown to be the largest psychiatric private practice in Kern County. S. A. Manohara, MD, FAPA, practices psychiatry and is a board-certified psychiatrist in addiction, forensic, and geriatric psychiatry. Dr. Manohara is well known in the medical community for his expertise in psychiatry.

As an expert in neuropsychology, I have had the pleasure of discussion and friendly debate about many of the things I have questioned and been taught about my own personal faith as a Christian and my practice as a forensic neuropsychologist. My doctorate in psychology at Rosemead School of Psychology at Biola University in the early 1970s focused on integrating psychology and theology. Of course, it had a Christian emphasis, as it should have.

Dr. Manohara, a devout Hindu, was open to my personal perspective and my own unique oneness. I soon realized he was extremely intelligent and open minded, and I looked forward to our numerous discussions about life, religion, science, and psychiatry. This book brings together many of the thoughts and ideas we discussed over the decades.

We had many thought-provoking discussions over the past three decades regarding human nature, mental health, and the healing of a mental disorder. Dr. Manohara has finished writing the book he promised as he attempted to explain to me the focus and commonality of many of those discussions. In this book the reader has the opportunity to experience and enjoy these thought-provoking conversations.

Hopefully the reader has had the opportunity to read the Freud-Jung letters because many of the conversations Dr. Manohara and I have had over the years remind me of those letters. Dr. Freud and Dr. Jung, as they corresponded in those letters, shared their agreements and conflict regarding human nature and mental health. Dr. Freud and Dr. Jung discussed in great detail their understanding of a spiritual nature or nonspiritual nature of man involved in their psychiatric practices. One of my favorite comparisons in the Freud-Jung letters was that Dr. Freud told Dr. Jung, who had recently studied and traveled in India, that he had been one of his very best students until he believed in God. As a result, Dr. Jung posted a sign above the threshold of his home, saying, "Called or uncalled God is always present" as a final word to Dr. Freud when he came to visit.

In this book, Dr. Manohara's explanation of the differences between Sigmund Freud and Carl Jung is brought together in their description of the ego. Dr. Manohara points out that the ego concept Dr. Freud and Dr. Jung were describing essentially provided the final pathway through which perception reaches reality formation through the executive functioning of the brain.

Dr. Manohara discusses how inaccurate perception is what leads to hallucinations, delusions, paranoia, and other inaccurate perceptual states. He also shares that this is the fundamental foundation of the unique oneness theory.

As a neuropsychiatrist and philosopher, Dr. Manohara brings the understanding of unique oneness theory in both a scientific and personal way. He explains in a very comprehensive approach how we scientist believers define reality, awareness, consciousness, and perception. His explanation of consciousness divided into two parts—with an inner consciousness that is subjective and responsible for the awareness of self and an outer consciousness that is objective and responsible for the awareness of one's outer world—is very thought provoking.

One thing I often share with patients is that another's perception is their reality. However, that reality may not compute with your perceptions, and therefore you have a challenge in communicating with one another. Empathy requires that we are able to understand each other's perceptions, which create our own personal reality. In this book Dr. Manohara points out that we are all unique in our own perceptions, which are also different compared to one another's unique perceptions and realities.

The reader will enjoy Dr. Manohara's theory as a novel look at human perception with direct application to human understanding and treatment. Oneness and absolute truth are described and explained in such a fashion through the history of psychiatry and the understanding of the psyche. As a result, unique oneness theory could also be used to comprehend our current understanding of humanity.

In this book, from the connection of the development of our frontal lobes in our brains came the idea of humans being able to think about thinking, which leads us to the concept of something or someone larger than ourselves. Referring to Albert Einstein's conclusion that religion at its highest form accommodates scientific fact into its beliefs as truth bridges the gap between science and religion. Scientific truth that is first rejected as conflicting with our faith has an impact on our own personal perceptions. Unique oneness theory explains the process of perception and offers answers to the mysteries of one's self-awareness of reality perceived where science fails. In this regard theology meets science.

Dr. Manohara acknowledges that there is a dichotomy between science and religion as he explains how science and religion resolve those differences. Unique oneness theory illuminates what lies between science and religion. He argues that if truly only one reality exists, then science and religion will eventually come together to make that one reality.

Unique oneness theory brings a comprehensive understanding that is useful in mental health treatment and intervention. In many ways it points out that we speak of similar human characteristics from different perceptions and languages, but they must come together; thus, we have unique oneness theory.

It is with great pleasure that Dr. Manohara asked me to write the foreword for his book on unique oneness theory. I predict that this book will be sought out as an excellent reference for students and professionals in the field of mental health. In this global understanding of the whole person, Dr. Manohara has provided a gift for those who wish to understand.

Dean Haddock, PsyD, ABMP, BCFE, BCME, ABDA
Clinical Psychologist PSY 8536

CHAPTER 1

A Need for a New Perspective

Imagine the paradigm shift that occurred when Galileo defended the heliocentric theory of the solar system Copernicus proposed. Despite the Catholic Church's aggressive attack, he stuck to his beliefs, offering his observed changes in the tides as evidence of his beliefs. Today, of course, we take the heliocentric perspective for granted as being the accepted view of our galaxy. Imagine the paradigm shift when by Antonie van Leeuwenhoek first discovered red blood cells and bacteria under the microscope. Despite some initial resistance in accepting his discoveries, his findings were eventually accepted. The discovery, of course, revolutionized how germs and disease have since been approached.

In this light, it's not difficult to appreciate how shortcomings still exist in many facets of science and medicine. Research for a cure for cancer, the ability to formulate DNA-based treatments for genetic disorders, and other research endeavors for obscure medical solutions persist in the vacuum of seemingly endless perplexities. It is within this framework that a fresh perspective on how our minds function is offered. Despite all we have discovered about the human nervous system, so much remains unanswered. We seem to be just scratching the surface.

What we have learned thus far about the function of the brain has indeed been astounding. Our brains contain between ten and twenty million neurons, and these numbers don't include the much larger number of non-neuronal brain cells. And while the function of these neurons and other brain cells is somewhat understood, their entire array of functions remains quite elusive. Each of these neurons has thousands of interconnections with other neurons and other cells. The resultant neural network encompasses hundreds of trillions of connections, through which mental processing occurs. Depending on which pathway is stimulated, an almost infinite number of results can take place. This fact alone humbles the most dedicated theorist and medical researcher.

It is a modern-day understanding that these neurons communicate through various electrical impulses and through the release of chemicals called "neurotransmitters." And a large amount of information is known about the brain's anatomy, chemistry, physiology, and interaction with other systems. However, the ability to account for human behavior and perception has yet to be well explained despite current knowledge. Theories have so far fallen short of explaining how we perceive the world around us and what we know to be our own personal selves.

The theory of evolution cannot easily explain the development of complex human organs, such as the eyes. Quantum mechanics cannot explain the human mind or human consciousness or the macroscopic aspects of the universe.

The theory of relativity also has its own limitations. None of these theories can explain the unique behavior of human beings or the concept of ego or the self. The pursuit of mechanisms that absolutely determine observed outcomes has taken science a long way in understanding the laws of physics and the laws of nature.

The pursuit of mechanisms that absolutely determine observed outcomes has taken science a long way in understanding the laws of physics and laws of nature. But these fail when trying to account for observed reality.

On a basic level, we can look at how we perceive the world. With our current knowledge, we know an object with illumination of light projects an image on the retina through the lens of the eyes. From the retina, chemical changes occur that cause neurons to generate electrical signals along the optic nerve to other regions of the brain. These nerve projections then allow us to see the object in the external environment in terms of its size, color, spatial relation to other objects, and so forth. But despite these defined mechanisms, a mystery remains as to how one perceives an object and becomes aware of its existence.

According to our current understanding, the brain's perception is created through various information inputs it receives. Sensory input is assimilated from various sensory receptors, and the perception happens. But how does this phenomenon truly occur? And how does a person become aware that what is perceived is reality or unreality? And how does the seemingly unpredictable human behavior that results react to these perceptions? These are the areas where current science falls short.

The question arises regarding how the brain, physical stimuli, electrical impulses, and chemical reactions culminate into a perception of the outside world. Unique oneness theory has been created to help explain this process of perception.

For perception to be experienced, the brain must produce an exact replica of the outside world. Without the brain's ability to produce an exact replica of the external environment, perception cannot happen or will be significantly inaccurate. In fact, inaccurate perception is what leads to hallucinations, delusions, paranoia, and other states of misperception. This is the fundamental foundation of the unique oneness theory.

The second concept of the unique oneness theory pertains to the unification of objective reality and one's subjective experience. Perception can be accurate as described above, but if there is a failure to completely integrate this perception into subjective experience, the potential for perceptual dysfunction again exists. For the perception to be experienced as a true subjective experience, the subjective and objective must be meshed into one organic, inseparable unity.

The third concept of the theory pertains to the unique nature and experience every single person enjoys. The organic unity between subjective and objective experiences comes together to create a unique reality. In other words, the subjective and objective unification differs slightly for every person, thus making it unique. This unique reality, through which the perception is experienced for an individual, has almost unperceivable differences from the true external reality. And because each person's subjective experience is different, each person's perceived reality is unique for that person.

Scientists have recognized three states of consciousness: a state of wakefulness, a state of deep sleep, and a state where active dreaming takes place. Of these states of consciousness, two are actively engaged in using the perceptual system. In wakefulness, we perceive our actual external environments and incorporate these perceptions into our subjective experiences. However, in our active dream states, we are using our perceptual systems as well. The difference is that instead of using sensory input from the external environment to create a perception, internal brain stimuli from memories and experiences provide the stimuli to create the perception.

Just as each person's perception of reality is unique and unified with his or her subjective experience, each individual's dreams are unique for exactly the same reason. The only difference between active dreaming and wakefulness is the activation of external sensory stimuli and the level of awareness and consciousness present. In this manner, consciousness and awareness influence perception. And in fact, the same perception of self and ego is influenced by these factors as well. Each of these will be defined in greater detail in subsequent chapters and integrated into unique oneness theory.

Unique oneness theory will also explore how to explain healthy human functioning. Insight can be obtained into many medical conditions by applying the theory's features to pathological states. Potential applications of this theory related to several common psychiatric and neurologic disorders—such as schizophrenia, Alzheimer's dementia, and autistic spectrum disorders—can be more easily understood in the light of an altered perceptual system.

With a new framework in perspective, different techniques in prevention and treatment can be developed. Changes in psychotherapy, medication, and research methods can be incorporated into new theoretical approaches. These then broaden the scope through which many individuals can be helped.

To provide a rationale for unique oneness theory, the subsequent section will provide key definitions and concepts to help understand the current state of scientific and medical concepts regarding the function of the brain. In doing so, weaknesses in our current knowledge will be discussed in greater depth, and the way unique oneness theory can help fill these voids will be described. While this discussion will certainly detail perceptual systems, various sections will also cover more broad-reaching considerations.

Unique oneness theory will also attempt to bridge the gaps of knowledge in quantum mechanics, evolutionary theory, and the theory of relativity. In doing so, the hope is to develop a unified theory involving matter, mind, and the brain; and to explore how these interact with consciousness. Concepts of mechanistic and nonmechanistic components will be considered, which will provide new ways to assess the roles the mind and brain serve and how they function in defining individual reality.

Unique oneness theory offers a new look at how the brain and mental processes explain how one perceives and relates to the world and the internal self. At the same time, it opens doors for new possibilities in describing how the brain functions, how awareness is realized, and how mechanistic properties of matter may interact with nonmechanistic entities to achieve a more comprehensive view of human consciousness.

When we allow a new perspective to take place, other opportunities to address health and wellness become available, where current medical theories and practices have reached roadblocks. A paradigm shift is needed to reach a greater understanding of human functioning to surpass these obstacles. In return, even greater understanding can then follow. It is within this light that the theory of unique oneness will be presented.

CHAPTER 2

Laying the Groundwork

In certain individuals suffering from Alzheimer's dementia, visual and auditory hallucinations are a prominent symptom during more advanced stages of the disease. As neurofibrillary tangles and amyloid plaques develop and disrupt the normal neural networks of millions of neurons, misperceptions about the external world begin to force their way into the person's consciousness. For example, the patient perceives a pink cat running across the bedroom floor. What appears to be real and thus part of reality is simply generated from within the brain. But for the sufferer of the hallucination, the ability to distinguish this from everyone else's reality is impossible.

Unique oneness theory seeks to explain this phenomenon by describing how the brain generates perceptions. But to speak in a systemized way about this and other facets of the theory, some groundwork regarding key definitions must be laid. What defines reality? What is consciousness? What is considered the ego and the self? Without a clear understanding of what these terms represent, discussions can quickly become very confusing. At the same time, these same definitions are crucial in accounting for differences between normal and pathological states.

For example, the same pink cat running across a bedroom floor may be part of a dream during REM sleep. Is this a hallucination? Of course not. This is a dream image also generated by our brains' perceptual system, but it's part of an altered state of consciousness we know as sleep. In contrast, the same image for an Alzheimer's patient while awake is pathological (assuming a pink cat didn't actually run across the bedroom floor). Defining terms allows us to understand why one is normal and one is not; and it allows us to identify better insights on how our brains function.

In the following, how we define reality, awareness, consciousness, and perception will be discussed. These terms have broad meanings that extend well beyond the scope of clinical medicine. But these extended definitions offer some important considerations in exploring new theories of mental processing and the brain's interaction with the environment. Rather than a strict mechanistic explanation of neuronal synapses and the release of neurotransmitters, more expansive definitions of such terms provide opportunities to explore nonmechanistic associations.

How these concepts relate to brain processes and to what we perceive as the ego and self is also important. After all, being able to accurately perceive self and nonself is a key part of defining reality for an individual. Once these interactions are better understood, aberrations of these normal relationships can then be considered in various disorders. By knowing how normal associations take place, theories between abnormalities and symptoms can be postulated along with therapeutic interventions. While this is the primary purpose of unique oneness theory, its role in gaining a more complete and unified insight into human complexities is certainly advantageous for future understandings.

Defining *Reality*

By simplistic terms, reality is what is real. And what is real is what exists. Reality is therefore a state of things as they actually are, and it equates to existence. But in considering the nuances of this simple definition, some very important considerations must be taken into account. For example, does something have to be observed or comprehended to exist and be part of reality? Or can reality encompass what is unable to be observed and understood? Likewise, is reality some form of absolute existence? Or does reality vary from individual to individual based on perception and interpretation?

Philosopher Edward Husserl popularized phenomenological reality in the early twentieth century. This basically defines reality as a personal interpretation of events as one person sees them. In essence, each person's reality differs according to his or her perception and interpretation. Phenomenological reality is used to explain certain spiritual experiences among individuals since not everyone may experience or perceive them, yet they are very real to those experiencing them.

In contrast, the concept of realism holds that a reality exists that is independent of the beliefs, perceptions, or experiences of an individual or a group of people. In other words, regardless of whether something is observed or able to be comprehended, there is an existence and a reality that is present regardless. Perception isn't required for the reality to be "real." This type of reality definition states that there is an identical reality for everyone, but differences in perception and interpretations create unique variations for each person.

In coming to a definition of *reality*, two basic features come into play. First is the nature of reality and whether it is absolute or relative to the one observing it. And second, to what extent does the relationship between the mind and reality affect defined reality? The proverbial question of "If a tree falls in the woods and no one is around to see it, does the tree actually fall?" highlights this key point in how one defines reality.

In more recent times, the theories of quantum physics define the properties of matter and energy within the universe. By nature, quantum physics concerns itself with probabilistic values rather than deterministic ones. This means an exact, determined answer to a set of circumstances isn't available in any particular instance, but instead a range of probabilities exists for various outcomes. In this regard, the universe is therefore nondeterministic and requires observation and consciousness to define reality. Outside our ability to observe and be aware of phenomenological occurrences, reality is simply an arbitrary concept.

The ultimate definition of reality depends on one's philosophical and scientific biases. Whether one tends to favor realism or prefers a phenomenological approach, ultimately reality can be determined to be somewhat different. Regardless, clearly our mental ability to perceive reality and render an interpretation of it requires our brain functions to operate normally. Without a functioning perceptual system, reality thus becomes distorted.

One could state that if reality is distorted because of pathological mental processing, then that simply is that person's reality. The different perceptions and interpretations lead to a different experience and thus redefine reality for that individual. This phenomenological approach to reality is interesting in this context. In what we don't know a great deal about healthy brain function, there is an abundance of medical evidence that demonstrates pathology causing distorted perceptions of reality. This includes hallucinations and delusions in an array of psychiatric illnesses.

For this reason, the definition of *reality* as used in unique oneness theory will focus on a view founded in realism. Unique oneness theory holds that individual perceptions and interpretations create personal differences in perceived reality. However, underlying this perceived reality is an absolute existence, on which this perceived reality is based. And that absolute existence is the one true reality. From this viewpoint, normal perceived reality at any given time is due to a combination of consensus perceptions as well as observed phenomenon. Similarly, pathologically perceived reality falls outside what is considered normal.

Because normal versus pathological perceptions are based on observations and consensus, these definitions change as observations and consensus change. For example, not long ago individuals who routinely slept only four hours a night were labeled insomniacs despite having no symptomatology. But scientifically we now know that a small percentage of the population requires only four hours of sleep nightly. Our perceived reality changes as our observations and interpretations change. But despite this fact, the underlying absolute reality isn't altered. These individuals were never insomniacs.

Similarly, the absolute reality that our solar system is heliocentric has always been in existence (at least since the origin of our galaxy). Our perception of a geocentric system didn't change the absolute reality but did alter phenomenological reality for people during the time prior of Copernicus. The absolute reality of infrared wavelengths and bacteria existed despite our inability to perceive these phenomena. Though in medicine we must work within a consensus of perceived reality to define normalcy, unique oneness theory will adhere to an underlying definition of reality as an absolute reality. This reality is the one we constantly seek to realize.

Defining *Consciousness*

Where do you start when defining *consciousness*? Philosophers, psychologists, and scientists have tried for centuries to capture a comprehensive definition for this topic. Yet agreements among various fields of study are far from cohesive. On a very basic level, *consciousness* means "awareness." To be conscious, one must be aware. But aware of what? A person is conscious of his or her environment, yet millions of brain processes are taking place, of which the person is unaware. Heartbeats, intestinal activity, vascular adjustments, and more all take place without any awareness at all. So, to some extent, this form of consciousness coexists with unconsciousness despite an awake or aware state of mind.

Clinically, medicine defines full consciousness as being awake, alert, and responsive to environmental stimuli. Lesser degrees of medical consciousness have reduced levels of these criteria until the other end of the spectrum is reached, which is a comatose state. Without question, science has provided significant support that this realm of consciousness resides within the functions of the brain. Mental processing enables alertness. Lesions involving various areas of the brain (brain stem, diencephalons, thalamus, and widespread cortical areas) reduce levels of alert consciousness, as do drugs and medications that suppress these brain areas. Functional imaging supports this further.

However, in trying to reach a more in-depth understanding of consciousness, medical definitions fall short in many ways. Philosophical and psychological definitions begin to award other qualities to consciousness other than simply an alert mental state. In this light, consciousness involves not only an alert mind but also an ability to recognize self and inner sentient states. This expands the objective orientation of awareness to a subjective realm that relates not only to the environment but also to the individual.

With this in mind, consciousness can be divided into two parts: an inner consciousness that is subjective and responsible for the awareness of self and an outer consciousness that is objective and responsible for the awareness of the world and the external environment. The concept of self, which will be defined subsequently, requires consciousness to exist. In fact, self serves to accurately distinguish between the inner and outer aspects of consciousness.

So far, the definitions of *consciousness* have focused on functions of the brain. From the medical definition, mental processes that allow alertness and external awareness have been described. Psychologically, the ability to recognize self and nonself portrays another aspect of consciousness. But in addition to these mental functions, other philosophical perspectives on consciousness exist outside the realm of the brain and nervous system. This aspect of consciousness deals with the ability to appreciate what is actual mental activity and what isn't.

Many philosophical viewpoints and religions describe consciousness as awareness not only of matter, thoughts, and emotions but also of awareness of nonmental aspects. *Spiritual* has been used as the most common term in labeling this aspect of consciousness. Of all the definitions of consciousness, this area is the one that is most controversial. Scientists and medical theorists most commonly hold a belief that consciousness solely arises from within the vast neural networks of the brain. Others strongly believe that consciousness arises from outside the brain matter yet is intimately connected with mental function. This interconnection between form and formlessness, matter and spirit, is ultimately what constitutes full consciousness in this definition.

Let me elucidate this latter viewpoint of consciousness; the mind is thought to be a tool consciousness uses to seek reality and define self. This reality is the absolute reality that has been defined previously rather than simply and individual's perceived reality. Because this higher consciousness is separate from mental function, the ability to appreciate absolute reality exists outside what can be observed and interpreted completely. The mind can therefore be used to facilitate a deepening of inner consciousness by introspection or can focus on outer consciousness through external sensory perception and thought.

Within the context of unique oneness theory, consciousness predominantly involves the ability to perceive external form and to distinguish between self and nonself. This awareness allows perception to occur just as light allows the eyes to see objects. And though an absolute reality exists, individual consciousness perceives a unique version of this reality that is specific to that individual. This is what creates a unique perception. Because the sensory systems and mental functions of an individual are individualized, the reality of perceptual experience is unique.

At the same time, consciousness enables both a unification and a separation between self and nonself, internal and external, form and formless. Discriminative abilities of the mind allow separation in perception, but one cannot exist without the other. In other words, form requires space (or formlessness) to be perceived. The external environment is given meaning by contrasting this with self and internal systems. Consciousness therefore provides unification between these dualistic entities. So while each individual's experience is unique, consciousness and absolute reality provide a "oneness" to all perceptions and experiences.

Defining *Perception*

Compared to reality and consciousness, perception is slightly less abstract but not necessarily less confusing in its definition. Perception is the awareness and understanding of sensory information. Though simple in its basic definition, perception occurrences are through mechanisms that are far from simplistic. From having multiple forms of sensory input to the means by which perception then occurs, these mechanisms appear to be very complex.

First, sensory stimuli and input are quite varied. Touch, sight, smell, taste, and hearing are receptive means by which the brain receives sensory information. But in addition, our brains receive information from movement and motor function as well. How our bodies move in space provides constant feedback about the environment and our bodies. However, perception isn't simply receiving information input in our brains. Once received, our existing mental concepts, thoughts, and emotions then influence the perception that occurs.

Some of the mental concepts that affect perception include experiences, cultural beliefs, and even sensory thresholds for information. Experiences and beliefs create biases and preconceptions that taint how information is perceived. For example, a person trained in the military for many years may have no difficulty detecting camouflage apparel, while someone unaware of such clothing may be unable to perceive it in a wooded environment. Preconceived emotions about a potential situation may automatically taint how the situation is perceived when it indeed occurs. This causes individual perceptual differences among each of us.

Sensory thresholds are likewise important. A disorder affecting sensory abilities will affect how well a person is able to perceive the environment or one's own body A result is only as good as the information input into the system. By the same token, if a person has never before experienced a situation or event, the ability to perceive it may be impossible. This can occur at a simplistic perceptual level but occurs with greater frequency as perceptions become more complex. The ability to understand and perceive the definitions outlined in this chapter, in fact, require an ability to read, understand a specific language, and have some ability to perceive complex concepts.

From this explanation, it isn't hard to appreciate that unique perceptions occur for each person. On a more basic level, unique oneness theory addresses how a person initially perceives the external world. The ability to accurately perceive the external environment is naturally dependent on the ability to receive accurate sensory input. The brain must first receive factual information about various aspects of the world in which it exists. This is the first step in our minds' perceptual system.

Subsequently, the brain must assimilate this information into some type of mind concept to base its perception of the world. As mentioned, actual events in the worlds aren't perceived in real time. There is an inherent delay between the actual occurrence of an event and when the brain perceives the event. Because of this, it is intuitive that the brain must have an inner perceptual system where its external world is recreated. In other words, the mind creates a virtual reality of the absolute external reality so it may perceive it.

Once the brain assimilates this information, beliefs, emotions, and thoughts then influence how the perception is fully processed. A person who has known only peace, love, and benevolence may view a situation completely different from someone who has known only violence and injustice. At a basic level, their perceptions may be very similar, but at a more complex level, their perceptions are remarkably unique and different.

Appreciating that perception is very individualized and internalized is an important part. The ability to perceive the world, one's own body, and even internal consciousness is a function of the brain. Without mental processes, the ability to receive, assimilate, and interpret information and thus allow perception would be lost. The intricate and almost countless neural networks provide a means by which we can perceive many things with tremendous accuracy. But at the same time, despite this incredible accuracy, perceptions still have inherent misperceptions when compared to absolute reality.

In this regard, the mind is the seat of perception. However, the mind isn't the seat of absolute reality or internal consciousness. These entities are intimately connected to our perceptions and our minds, but at the same time they are separate. These are the characteristics that create both a uniqueness and a oneness to human experience.

Defining *Self*

Like consciousness, defining self has some of the same difficulties depending on the perspective with which you view the concept. *Self* generally is defined as one's own identity ... but what defines one's identity? From a psychological perspective, self and identity are used synonymously with personality. Personality then includes all the cognitive and affective aspects of one's existence. On the surface, self would then seem to reflect the outcomes of mental activity alone and be harbored within the brain.

In considering the definitions of *perception*, this assumption that the seat of self resides within the mind wouldn't necessarily be correct. The brain is used to enable perception of internal and external consciousness, and it is the tool by which thoughts and emotions are interpreted. However, the mind needs only to allow perception of self through its abilities. The mind doesn't have to contain self in total.

According to Carl Jung, personality encompasses ego, consciousness, and unconsciousness. And at the center of personality is self; ego, on the other hand, is located at the center of consciousness. Therefore, self is defined as representing a much broader and all-encompassing concept compared to the ego. In Jung's definitions, the term *consciousness* is used in the psychological sense, reflecting the mind's awareness, not the more global philosophical connotation.

Without question, self involves thoughts, emotions, and behaviors of an individual, which are reflective of personality. The area where some disagree is whether a nonmental aspect of self exists. Does this nonmental aspect add to one's personality, or are self and personality only by-products of the mind? This becomes a philosophical question. In essence, the answer lies in whether consciousness is viewed as having a nonmental aspect. This difference in opinion regarding consciousness has been discussed.

For purposes of unique oneness theory, *self* needs be defined as only an individual's own reflective consciousness. Whether that reflection comes from only the mind or from nonmental sources as well isn't significant for purposes of the discussion on self. From a practical standpoint, self represents an individual's personality and identity, which are unique to that person. Personality is thus the combination of many things, which clearly include perception and mental activities. And personality may include additional aspects that reflect nonmental activities.

Regardless, self is the part that makes each of us unique and distinct from one another. Self also distinguishes between what is subjective and part of one's own identity, and what is objective and part of the external environment. In order words, self is reflective of one's inner consciousness in contrast to outer consciousness. Perception plays an integral part in this determination, which has been outlined. The other major component involved in this determination is the ego.

Defining *Ego*

Ego is a commonly used term today for a variety of references. In everyday speech, the ego often refers to one's sense of pride or individual superiority; however, psychologically speaking, ego has a different meaning. The ego defined in the realm of psychology serves an executive function of the brain to organize and explain reality. In other words, the ego makes rational sense of the perceived world.

Aspects assigned to the ego have included cognitive abilities, perceptual interpretations, defensive rationalizations, and overall executive functions. The ego takes the perceptions of the mind and accommodates them into an organized, rational form of reality an individual can accept. Of course, this depends on the individual. Each person has different ways of rationalizing perceptions, and each has different variations of perceived reality. Once the ego has assimilated this information into a working format, the individual can then react and respond.

In contrast to Jung, who stated that ego was at the center of consciousness, Sigmund Freud suggested that ego had both conscious and unconscious aspects. Again, the reference to consciousness is better defined as awareness in these contexts. The ego is constantly organizing and defining reality based on a person's experiences, cultural beliefs, and perceptions, regardless of whether he or she is aware of this. In this manner, the ego acts out underlying psychological disturbances the individual may not fully understand. This is the unconscious aspect of the ego, which Freud described.

In short, the ego defines reality for a person. The ego resolves conflicts between instincts, environment, and conscience using the tools of the mind it has at its disposal. In addition, the ego binds the self to its physical body and certain aspects of the external world. For example, the ego accurately defines possession of an automobile or a house to one's self as it does to its own limbs, eyes, and so forth. A poorly functional ego then can lead to dysfunctions in the perception of self and the external environment as well as perceptual aberrations.

From the perspective of consciousness, those who view consciousness as having mental and nonmental characteristics (physical and spiritual may be another description of this delineation), the ego serves a role in bridging inner consciousness to outer consciousness. In other words, the ego uses mental functions not only to distinguish the inner self from the external environment but also to link nonmental and mental functions in creating human behavior. From this perspective, the ego (like the mind) is a tool the self uses to know itself. By relating inner consciousness and outer consciousness, the self gains complete view of its identity.

Unique oneness theory holds that the ego serves an important role in perceptual abilities of the mind. The ego takes perceived input, and through executive functions, it makes sense of the information. In addition, the ego uses existing information, such as memories, emotional biases, cultural beliefs, and even self-reflective consciousness to determine what the individual ultimately defines as reality. The perceived reality via the ego changes as any of these input variables change. Thus, there is a unified consensus of reality for the individual that is unique to that individual. The ego essentially provides the final pathway, through which perception reaches reality formation.

By reviewing the concepts of consciousness, reality, perception, self, and ego, some understanding is possible in relating these to human function. However, at the same time, differences in opinion and theory make absolute definitions impossible without further consensus or proof. Given the limits of our collective understanding of the mind's ability to process information, a widespread understanding of terms such as *consciousness* is unlikely to occur anytime soon. In fact, some believe we will never know consciousness because what is sought and the seeker are one and the same.

Regardless of an agreed-upon consensus, working definitions for these terms are helpful when describing theoretical models.

One may adopt different definitions according to one's own reality processing and apply them to a proposed theory. In the case of unique oneness theory, loose definitions are adequate, especially when using terms such as *consciousness* and *self*. However, for terms such as *perception reality* and *ego*, more concrete definitions are needed to appreciate the nuances of the theory's hypotheses. It's within these areas that one can understand both the unification and uniqueness that develop for each of us.

Having stated this, I must add that the ability to consider philosophical aspects of consciousness and self awards greater potential to unique oneness theory. Much of the current scientific limitations in understanding the workings of the mind and self, consciousness and unconsciousness, and matter versus nonmatter come from limitations in current theories. Both deterministic theories and probabilistic theories fall short in explaining human behavior. This may mean that new perspectives need to be embraced to gain greater understanding.

A paradigm shift may be needed for us to accurately perceive absolute reality to a greater extent. If our current beliefs and preconceived limitations prevent the mind from perceiving reality accurately, theories of quantum physics may actually hinder a greater understanding of the human mind and body more than they help. Unique oneness theory provides a means by which new perspectives can occur and thus allow more accurate perceptions to take place.

With this in mind, we will look at some of the philosophical considerations that influence how we perceive the workings of the mind and view self and consciousness. While unique oneness theory doesn't adhere to any specific philosophical viewpoint in this regard, it does open the door for considering new aspects of how consciousness influences perception, personality self, and unique realities. Through this discussion, new approaches to both normal and pathological mental functions can be developed.

CHAPTER 3

Various Theories of Perception

Given the complexity of the subject matter and its abstract nature, definitions of *consciousness*, *perception*, and *awareness* have been debated through the centuries and continue to be debated today. As we learn more about what's human and psychology, new facts can help mold more accurate definitions and concepts. In fact, this is exactly how perception gives rise to knowledge and beliefs over time.

From the earliest scientists and philosophers, considerations of how perception occurs have been of great interest. Remarkably, some of the earliest theories of perception and consciousness hold many truths despite the lack of objective science to support them at the time. A common thread runs through many theories about how perception works and how it relates to consciousness and self. But, at the same time, some key differences in opinion are evident as well.

In this chapter, philosophical and historical considerations will be discussed to help clarify the details of unique oneness theory more thoroughly. In doing so, specific areas of similarities and contrasts will be highlighted.

Perception according to Aristotle

Aristotle was a master of science and philosophy during his time. It's no surprise that his written works addressed the issues of perception and how the perceptual process took place. Like many philosophers to follow him, however, Aristotle's theory fell into an abstract realm, since many details and facts about human anatomy and physiology were centuries away. Despite this handicap, Aristotle interestingly contemplated some important aspects regarding perception.

In his work *De Anima*, Aristotle explained perception as an event of the sense organs. But for him, the sense organs weren't the well-known nerve endings for touch, the taste buds for taste, the retina for sight, and so forth. Instead, the sense organs consisted of two basic elements: air and water. For example, if a noise occurred in the environment, the noise was transmitted through the basis medium of air to arrive to the body. Or through the medium of water, tastes were transmitted to the mouth. Air and water were the integral media through which sensations could be received.

But what exactly was the sense organ? For Aristotle, air and water were the elements of the sense organ. The manner by which the body perceived an object required the medium to become a likeness of the object perceived. If an apple was the object in the external environment, the air medium would adopt a form like the apple and transmit this precept through the eye. Air in essence was the sense organ for vision.

It is noteworthy that Aristotle, while not having the benefit of neuroanatomy knowledge, proposed that perception occurred indirectly. Like other philosophers and unique oneness theory, the actual reality wasn't directly perceived but instead was indirectly perceived. While Aristotle proposed that an elemental medium adopt a form of the actual reality to be perceived, unique oneness theory uses what is now known about the brain to propose the same phenomenon. The difference is that current-day knowledge regarding neurophysiology is incorporated into unique oneness theory. Instead of air taking on the form of the apple and transmitting this image to the body, the image is relayed through the retina via neural pathways and eventually creates a mental image of the apple in the mind.

The other noteworthy aspect of Aristotle's theories was his belief that physiological aspects of perception resided within the body; however; psychological aspects of perception resided within the soul. In other words, objects could be sensed within the environment through the body's interaction with sense organs. But the ability to form concepts and gain knowledge about that object required the soul to construct a more complex perception. Like subsequent philosophers, Aristotle postulated a two-tiered perceptual system.

Aristotle believed that the ability to perceive was what separated animals from plants. On a basic level, he stated that animals needed to touch, taste, smell, and so forth to find food and survive. But as the complexity of animals reached greater hierarchy, perception provided not only needed skills for survival but also abilities to enjoy the goodness of life. Complexity of perception was therefore associated with mankind and distinguished man from other animals.

As other scientists' and philosophers' theories of reality, perception, and knowledge are discussed, it will become apparent that Aristotle covered many of the central tenets lying at the heart of the debate. Is perception a direct or indirect process of reality's interpretation? How many tiers of complexity exist between basic perception and knowledge? How does human perception differ from animal perception? How do perception, the soul, and consciousness interact? His theories offer a great foundation from which to discuss the evolution of these theories.

Perception according to Descartes

René Descartes, a French philosopher and scientist of the seventeenth century, pondered not only perception and reality but also existence itself. In several writings, listed as *Meditations*, Descartes proceeded through a rational series of thoughts and deductions about God, the nature of reality, and human existence. Descartes came to the conclusion in his first meditation that because he was, he therefore indeed existed. From there, he came to accept that "I think, therefore I exist."

Descartes equated thinking with the mind, intellect, understanding, reason, and even the soul. The seat of the soul resided in the mind, according to his philosophy. It is no wonder that perception was located somewhere other than the mind, while equating consciousness, awareness, and existence to thinking would be difficult at best. The bigger issue, however, for Descartes was whether perception examined reality.

In essence, Descartes believed three possibilities existed for perception. The first was considered adventitious, which meant perception was based on the outside world. Second, perception could be factitious, meaning that perceptual ideas originated from within the mind. Finally, perceptions could be innate, which meant they were inscribed by God or a supreme being. Ultimately, Descartes concluded that matter was adventitious in perception and based on an external reality.

Like Aristotle, he believed in an indirect perceptual system, where sensory information was received about the environment through sense organs. This allowed realization about the external world to take place. However, unlike Aristotle, Descartes believed the mind was the only organ to sense perception. In this manner, Descartes described a mind-body dualism, in which the mind represented a single, unitary organ that was indivisible. Unlike the body, which could be dissected, he viewed the mind as nonfunctional unless whole.

The process of perception consisted of two tiers. The first level consisted of the senses providing information about corporeal things of matter. The mind then received this information and provided true perception and understanding. Because the mind was the seat of everything, the body offered little but a relay of data for processing. Likewise, the soul was part of thinking and thus associated with the mind as part of its unity.

Descartes provided wax in its solid and liquid forms as examples of how the body could sense the different forms, but only the mind could perceive the association between the two forms and link them together as the same compound. This accounted for perception in his theory.

While much of Descartes's theories are intriguing, the fact that the mind can function in part after various injuries, tumors, and pathologies makes his indivisibility of the mind less valid. Descartes also didn't have the benefit of knowledge about neuroanatomy and neurophysiology, which evolved within the last century. Despite this lack, his indivisibility of the mind provides a platform for the immortality and unity of the soul and an overriding unity of reality. In this way, the oneness of unique oneness theory and some of Descartes's views can be compared.

Perception according to Locke

John Locke, a seventeenth-century English philosopher, had a profound impact through the Enlightenment period. Like Aristotle and Descartes, his opinions regarding perception adopted an indirect approach. The perception of an object was mediated through sensory information but didn't directly proceed from object to awareness. However, unlike the other philosophers described, Locke defined *perception* somewhat differently.

Others before Locke had described indirect perception as a two-tiered system, where perception began as sensory informational input on one level, then proceeded to be realized as perceptions as other organs processed the information. In other words, the first tier was the receipt of perceptual data, and the second was awareness of the perception. For Descartes this second tier occurred at the level of the mind. For Aristotle, this occurred at the level of the soul. But for Locke, perception occurred immediately and simultaneously as a single tier.

The key difference was that Locke viewed an idea of the mind as being a perception, thought, or understanding. Each of these was an immediate object of mental activity. The act of receiving sensory information about one's environment or body immediately generated an idea of perception. For example, the perception (or idea) of an apple occurred immediately when the image was received from visual input to the eye. The need of several steps to occur between the sensory information and the idea wasn't felt to be necessary.

However, perceptual knowledge, according to Locke, was different. Perceptual knowledge occurred when conformity existed between ideas and the environment. Rather than a single cause-and-effect occurrence between an object and its perception, perceptual knowledge judged the conformity among several ideas. Since an idea could be a perception, thought, or understanding, perceptual knowledge included memories, existing knowledge and biases, and so forth. The immediate perception that occurred didn't require conceptualization and judgment; however, perceptual knowledge did.

The aspect of judgment Locke described is worth noting from the perspective of unique oneness theory. Judgment acting on a perception, according to Locke, was a process in which ideas were constantly being changed to create new knowledge or mold existing knowledge. This imparted flexibility to the system. Similarly, unique oneness theory highlights this same flexibility in the perceptual system, which is what makes each of us unique. We perceive reality in slightly different ways, and this perception is undergoing constant adjustments.

Locke realized the external environment, which is ultimate reality in unique oneness theory, wasn't accurately perceived to perfection as ideas and knowledge were formed. Instead, a constant state of flux was ongoing to create knowledge as close to reality and trust as possible given past and present perceptions, experiences, judgments, and discernment. Locke believed in the existence and reality of the objects being perceived, but in the perceptions process, error did occur.

While Descartes categorized everything in the form of cognitive thinking, Locke grouped everything in the form of an idea. But Descartes placed discernment and judgment within the thinking process, leading to complex tiers of perceptual interaction. Locke, on the other hand, only awarded the function of sensory organs and the awareness of this information in the perception process. Anything above this level, which involved discernment, was part of the act of gaining knowledge of reality.

Locke, in his description of how knowledge was gained, also didn't believe that innate knowledge existed. This belief was different from that of both Aristotle and Descartes, who felt a supreme being or God provided some innate knowledge and inscribed truths within the self. Locke, on the other hand, felt the self was both self-aware and self-reflective, and that the self through these processes achieved its own consciousness. This belief had profound influences on educational, parental, and scientific theories, subsequently even leading to current-day psychology methods. The power Locke awarded to the self and the concept of how knowledge was gained made great impact within many circles in the centuries to follow.

Perception according to Russell

Among other things, Bertrand Russell was an English philosopher, mathematician, and historian in the early portion of the twentieth century. His influences within the realm of perception occurred through his theories of how various cognitive aspects related to each other. These different aspects of cognition, according to Russell, included attention, sensation, memory, and imagination. The relationship of these determined how perceptions, concepts, and actual knowledge developed.

Russell used new terminology in describing his theories, and he specifically highlighted the term *acquaintance*. Acquaintance referred to the dual relationship between a subject and an object. An object could be a material form in the environment or a concept from within the mind. In defining these acquaintances, Russell noted the temporal relationship required when defining certain parts of cognition. For example, sensation and memory required temporal facets between subject and object in forming an acquaintance. In contrast, imagination required no such temporal relationship.

Perception was therefore defined as when an acquaintance formed between subject and object. Russell described three possible scenarios within the realm of perception. The first was materialistic monism, which defined reality as physical and real. In this case, mental phenomena were simple rearrangements of this physical matter in the mind. This indirect perceptual theory was like other theories, but Russell criticized it because it failed to account for abstract form or imagination.

The second scenario was defined as idealistic monism. In this case, like Descartes's fictitious category, all reality was derived from mental activity, and all physical matter was actually produced by the mind. Russell criticized this possibility for its inability to allow the subject to directly experience an external environment. Though his method was not as elaborate as Descartes's investigation into the subject, Russell felt that some form of external reality indeed existed.

Third, Russell described neutral monism, which gave credence to both physical and mental relations. In this case, both physical and mental realities were based on a separate neutral element so neither was inherently perfect. However, because both were based on a single neutral element, both physical and mental realities weren't instinctively different. Russell criticized this possibility due to its inability to distinguish mental from physical perceptions and their relationship to the true reality.

Russell was a monist (he believed in monism) like the other philosophers already mentioned. Monism adheres to the concept that there is one underlying reality and that all perception is based on this one entity. However, Russell resolved his criticisms by accepting that an ongoing relationship between physical and mental realities existed, thus creating acquaintances. These acquaintances led to the trust that was the ultimate reality. In this way, all the cognitive realms described, including imagination and attention, could be accounted for within a realistic, monistic structure.

To move from an acquaintance to a belief, multiple relations between a subject and a complex array of objects had to exist. In other words, a subject's beliefs developed through the occurrence of multiple acquaintances. Subsequently, once these beliefs became self-evident to the subject, these beliefs then became truths that formed knowledge. The self-evident awareness of a belief provided justification within one's consciousness about that belief, transforming it into a trust and thus knowledge. As new acquaintances and beliefs were experienced through cognitive realms, trusts would be adjusted as would knowledge. Reality was thus always changing for a subject based on mental and physical perceptions as they led toward truths and knowledge.

Clear similarities exist between Russell's theories and unique oneness theory. The evolving relationship between subject and object Russell described is akin to the flexibility and uniqueness described in unique oneness theory. The subject in both instances has an ongoing state of flux, where knowledge is being refined as perceptions, beliefs, and truths that are being adjusted. These truths are subjective and not absolute. Therefore, these are subject to refinement while absolute truths are not. Perceptual experience progressively allows a subject to come to know ultimate reality more accurately.

The other main similarity is the monistic component. Like unique oneness theory, Russell believed in one ultimate reality, on which acquaintances were based between mental and physical entitles. This oneness, like absolute truths, is unchangeable and serves as a guide for evolving knowledge and beliefs. Perception for Russell was an indirect reflection of this oneness. In this manner, he shared commonalities with all monistic thinkers.

Perception according to Eastern Philosophers

Many different religious and spiritual perspectives exist regarding ultimate reality, consciousness, awareness, and the self. The scope of this book doesn't allow for each of the major religions to be detailed in this regard. However, some of the Eastern religions have specifically addressed perception as it pertains to reality. Some have offered unique insights into monism and the interaction between a person and his or her material environment.

Some of the earliest teachings of Hindus address some of these concepts. The Vedas, or Sanskrit, teachings were taught through the Vedanta school of Hindu philosophy. One of the sub-schools of the Vedanta was the Advaita Vedanta, which Adi Shankara described in a consolidated fashion. In this, Shankara addressed reality under the constructs of monism, raising the central difficulties that occur with all monistic theories.

The term *Advaita* means nondualism and inherently stresses oneness of ultimate reality. But within monism, which ascribed this oneness to everything real, the challenge is to account for the diversity of the world and the souls within the world under this umbrella. In other words, how does one reality or one God become so many? Within these ancient Indian teachings, this question was answered in two different ways.

According to Shankara, the diversity of the world and of souls within the world wasn't actually real. Instead, this was a phenomenon and an illusion created through perception. The actual reality was, in fact, one and undifferentiated. In other words, the diversity that appeared to exist was, in truth, undiversified. What was perceived as diverse actually wasn't. This doctrine of illusion is how Shankara accounted for the appearance of diversity while still adhering to the monistic foundation of the Vedanta.

In contrast to Shankara, another Indian philosopher named Ramanuja Acarya took a different approach. In a commentary regarding the Vedanta, which he titled the *Vedanta Sutra*, Ramanuja described reality and diversity from an alternate perspective. Like Shankara, Ramanuja agreed that ultimate reality was indeed a single oneness, and in this regard, he shared the monistic view. However, unlike Shankara, Ramanuja believed ultimate reality required differentiation to become absolute. In other words, absolute reality demanded differentiation to be perceived and realized. Ramanuja's philosophy was known as Visistadvaita, which was defined as oneness of organic unity but with differentiated monism. In essence, diversity and differentiation were required by absolute reality and rather were not an illusion of reality.

Ramanuja elaborated on this concept and described three fundamental categories of reality. These categories were God (*isvara*), soul (*cit*), and matter (*acit*). All three were part of the unity that defined reality. This meant that the world and the plurality of souls were part of reality as well. Additionally, all three were interconnected as one and organically related to each other.

God, as Ramanuja defined him, was the creator and the immanent ground of all existence. As such, God sustained and controlled souls and matter. In this way, souls and matter were dependent on God for their existence. But just as matter and souls were related in an organic way, so also was God to souls and matter. For example, the human soul was connected to the human body and the external world, and God was likewise connected to the human soul and matter in a similar fashion. None existed without the other. If souls and matter required God for existence, God required the differentiation of souls and matter to become absolute reality.

The importance of Ramanuja's concept of monism is the relationship between matter and the soul. This interconnection and intimate relationship offer a concept by which limitations in science today may be better explained. The mechanistic and deterministic aspects of science that link cause with effect in explaining how the world works are limited in their explanation of evolution and quantum physics. The laws of nature and physics (matter and energy) can go only so far in defining reality. However, if another entity, which wasn't material in nature, existed (the soul) and could interact with matter, influence matter, and thus be part of ultimate reality, then this could open many new areas of study and understanding. This nonmaterial entity wouldn't be subject to the same physical laws matter and energy are.

The limitations of mechanistic science will be described in a later chapter, but in terms of the perception of reality, Ramanuja offered a clear paradigm shift for what is accepted today as definitive science and medicine. For Ramanuja, multiple souls and a diversified world do indeed exist, yet all aspects of this diversification are unified as one absolute reality. Differentiation is therefore not an illusion, according to Ramanuja, but a necessity for reality to be fully perceived.

Perception and V. S. Ramachandran

Dr. V. S. Ramachandran, a renowned professor and neurologist, published extensively in the field of visual perception. As a lead professor at the University of California's San Diego Psychiatry Department and neurosciences program, his work in visual perceptual disorders has been revolutionary. For instance, he has used visual sensory feedback to help conditions such as phantom limb pain. Phantom limb pain describes a condition in which a person still perceives pain in a nonexistent limb after it has been amputated or lost. Ramachandran has used the brain's ability to change via different sensory inputs to treat such conditions.

Dr. Ramachandran has studied visual systems and perceptions during most of his career. It is, therefore, noteworthy to consider his theory of human perception. Having the benefit of modern neuroscience, his theories indeed consider a more scientific approach to perception and awareness. Information of neurochemistry and electrical neural connections enables hypotheses that perception an intricate encoded process. Through sensory inputs, data is collected to form abstractions and symbols within the brain. And with the help of billions of neurons present, high complexity processing of this data leads to conscious perception.

In considering other theories of perception, Ramachandran believes the simple transference of images of the environment to the brain doesn't solve the problem of how perception works. For example, the creation of a replica in the brain of the outer environment would still require that another 'little'man in the brain" perceive that internal replica. Likewise, that little man would need another smaller man to interpret his perceptual replica, and so on to infinity. Instead, Ramachandran believes the conversion of sensory data to symbols occurs at progressively more complex levels, eventually leading to human perception and awareness. In other words, perception and consciousness are fully seated in the brain and are completely physical in nature.

The limitations of Dr. Ramachandran's theory of perception are that the progressive dissection of data and information as well as subsequent recombinations of it into a complex pattern don't necessarily create awareness. If one saw an airplane flying across the sky, the ability of the visual system to dissect that sensory input into data that detailed color, shapes, and motions of the image is possible. But how does this data then get analyzed and reproduced into an awareness of that image with all its inherent meanings? In other words, how can physical analysis, regardless of how complex, provide a conscious perception of an event that is both physical and nonphysical in its content?

Even with billions of neurons and millions of neural networks, the ability of a physical system to reveal conscious awareness and perception hasn't been elucidated. Ramachandran supports that this is possible at a multitiered, highly complex level in the brain. While his theories support indirect perceptual systems, he awards conscious awareness to the brain solely without components of a soul or a nonphysical entity.

Like unique oneness theory, Ramachandran supports a unique perceptual ability for every human being since everyone's brain is unique. Likewise, neuroplasticity allows different sensory stimuli to alter perception, as he has demonstrated in his treatment of phantom limb conditions. Additionally, a presumed unification and oneness is present since the environment provides an absolute source, on which perception is based. It isn't clear how this absolute reality came to be, according to Ramachandran; regardless, its consistent reality and absolute character are presumed to be present in this theory.

The key difference between unique oneness theory and Ramachandran's theory of perception is how perception occurs. In the unique oneness theory, a perceptual image of the external environment is recreated through sensory stimuli in the mind by the perceptual systems of the brain. Then conscious awareness, a nonphysical entity, interprets this indirect perceptual image, providing a unique reality for the individual. In contrast, Ramachandran supposes this conscious awareness occurs through complex brain pathways, which repeatedly analyze data at multiple levels. To date, nothing has supported the position that this complex symbolic analysis allows awareness at any level.

Perception and Unique Oneness Theory

Like the philosophers, scientists, and spiritual teachers described, unique oneness theory shares two major facets with their opinions. One facet is the belief of monism, which holds that ultimate reality is a single, unified entity, and the other facet is the belief that perception is a process by which true reality reaches awareness through indirect means. Each of the above philosophies has components that are consistent with unique oneness theory and some that aren't. The recent advances in science and specifically neuroscience make some of the theories outdated. But even the ancient Hindu philosophies provide insights into perceptual processes in theory.

By ascribing to a unified monistic theory, oneness is embraced. This essentially means that a single ultimate reality exists. This reality is absolute and unchangeable from the perspective of unique oneness theory. The laws of nature and physics, which have defined the behavior of matter, are part of this absolute reality. However, the physical environment, which encompasses the world at large and the human body, isn't the only component of absolute reality. Other nonmaterial influences can also alter and change this physical world in certain circumstances. Likewise, the physical world can influence nonmaterial aspects of reality.

Without trying to establish a spiritual aspect of this nonmaterial component, the current focus of unique oneness theory is to address how each person has his or her own unique experience in the process of gaining knowledge about this ultimate reality. Each of us is constantly using sensory information to perceive our environment. Cognitive elements then process this information in the context of biases, memories, existing knowledge, and so forth to continually improve beliefs about reality. So despite perception being based on an absolute reality, the process of perception creates a flexible uniqueness special to each individual.

What we have come to understand from recent science is that this ability to adapt and be flexible in our perception of reality offers great potential in achieving better health. Neuroplasticity, which describes the brain's ability to change in response to internal and external stimuli, is a very real process. And children aren't the only ones who exhibit this capability. Just as a muscle responds to the type of exercise to which it is exposed, the neurons of the brain respond to various stimuli differently. In this way perceptual stimuli can alter beliefs, self-evident truths, and perspectives on reality. This fact opens the door for possible therapeutic uses of perception.

By our using unique oneness theory to explore the possibilities of mental, psychological, and medical therapies in treating various health conditions, new areas of exploration and research can evolve. In fact, pursing this to a great depth could even result in major scientific discoveries about how matter and energy interact with nonphysical matter and how energy interacts with nonphysical matter. Just as it's important for personal biases to be reduced or eliminated for one to accept a new aspect of reality, societal or organizational biases must be tossed aside if new perspectives can be achieved. These are the opportunities unique oneness theory offers.

Having explored philosophical histories about perception and reality, and expanded the understanding of unique oneness theory to a greater extent, we will now discuss the current understanding of neuroscience as it applies to our discussion. By grasping how the brain is currently known to function and interact with its environment, one can better appreciate not only what we know but also how much we still have to learn. Understanding areas of ignorance can help open one's mind to perceive new concepts and get a few steps closer to knowing ultimate reality.

CHAPTER 4

The Brain in the Twenty-First Century

Unlike Aristotle, Descartes, and other philosophers, who contemplated how the human mind achieved perception and awareness of its outer world, we today have a wealth of knowledge about the inner workings of the brain. However, even with our advanced knowledge of neurons, brain development neurophysiology, and more, most experts regard our knowledge as still being in its infancy. What we know about the brain's anatomy and function is astounding, and this alone has prompted many theorists to assume all perception, consciousness, and awareness reside in the confines of the nervous system.

Although we know a great deal about the brain, we don't understand nearly enough to make precise assumptions about all its functions and capabilities. However, what we do know can provide significant insight into what may be possible and impossible. From this perspective, knowing current aspects of the brain's anatomy and physiology can help create more accurate theories about human perception.

As a means to provide a current level of understanding about the human brain, details about its development anatomy and physiology will be described. Describing what is known about the brain will undoubtedly provide respect for its complexities, but at the same time, it will reveal some of its limitations in explaining perceptual awareness. These guiding principles based on current knowledge are what have led in part to the concepts of unique oneness theory. By having an appreciation of these principles, you will be able to comprehend the reasons behind the theory to a better extent and understand where other theories fall short.

In subsequent sections of this chapter, the development and anatomy of the brain will be described, while aspects of neurochemistry and input systems will be detailed in later chapters. This will provide a foundation on which to understand how the brain receives and processes perceptual information. Once this has been accomplished, thoughts about how this perceptual information reaches consciousness can be more easily considered.

Brain Development

From the moment of conception, a single cell proceeds to grow and expand through multiple divisions of it. Within three weeks, the beginnings of the brain and nervous system are already evident. A simple flat sheet of cells suddenly thickens in the middle to form a wrinkle, which then folds upon itself. This fold deepens and eventually forms a tube of cells as it falls beneath the surface of the embryo's body. Ultimately this tube develops into the brain and spinal cord. What was once on the outer surface of this cellular organism adjacent to the outer world becomes embedded in the body and self. Theoretically, this structure is therefore the ideal system to communicate the outer environment to the self through perceptual means.

What begins as just a few cells comprising the neural tube in the embryo gradually grows to be more than one hundred billion neurons of the mature brain and spinal cord over several months. And this figure doesn't include the other cells of the brain that provide neuronal support. During development and beyond, each neuron develops thousands of connections with other neurons, forming neural networks. The complexity of the nervous system becomes overwhelming in a short time when considering the magnitude of its intricacies.

The brain's development fortunately proceeds in a very organized fashion, allowing us to better grasp its very complex functions and anatomy. By taking a general overview of its anatomical organization as it relates to function, we can gain a better grasp of its nature. In essence, three key processes occur that provide a very specific plan, by which our nervous system develops.

The first process is the local development of the neurons and brain cells. Neurons within the neural tube (the enfolding) must migrate to the proper location of the nervous system to function properly. How does this process take place? Interestingly, single proteins in the nervous tissues trigger different neurons to express different genes. While all neurons at the start have a full complement of DNA material, only certain ones are turned "on." Specific gene expression stimulates some neurons to move upward toward the brain while others move downward toward the spinal cord. In a very detailed fashion, each neuron and brain cell reaches its anatomical destination by following the "road signs" these signal proteins and genes provide.

Once in place, neurons must then form connections with thousands of other neurons and cells. Each neuron undergoes what has been termed "morphogenesis." Morphogenesis describes the ability of a neuron to form outpouching, which ultimately grows into nerve fibers. Axons are nerve fibers that provide outgoing information from a neuron and can be several feet in length. Dendrites, on the other hand, are shorter and allow the neuron to receive incoming information. Through axons and dendrites, neurons interconnect with other cells and form vast, complex neural networks.

Much like a computer circuitry board, neuronal axons and dendrites create a web of communications throughout the nervous system. But how does such an organized structure occur? Within the tip of each axon and dendrite, a growth cone exists. Growth cones provide not only an engine for their growth to occur but also a steering mechanism to guide the structure to its destination.

At a not-so-blazing speed of one millimeter per day, nerve fibers move toward their end point as chemicals within the nervous tissue provide a map, which these growth cones follow. By moving along the same paths as other axons and dendrites, tight, organized nerve fiber bundles form. Just like bundles of electrical wire within an electronic machine, bundles of nerve fibers efficiently reach their target using the least amount of space and traveling the shortest distance.

Once a nerve fiber reaches its target tissues or cell, locally released chemicals in the target tissue provide feedback to the nerve fiber that it has successfully arrived. The chemicals, often called "neurotrophic factors," provide not only navigational feedback but also needed chemicals for sustenance and health of the nerve fiber. Despite this, more than half of all axons and dendrites eventually die as the neural network connections are refined. In other words, a built-in excess of neural connections is provided to ensure adequate numbers of nerve fibers reach their target tissues.

The final phase of neuronal development is an ongoing process that occurs throughout one's lifetime. Adjustment and refinement of neural connections, networks, axons, and dendrites are constantly occurring. Depending on which electrical and chemical signals a neuron receives, different changes occur within the cells. The brain is constantly adjusting to changes in its environment.

The term *neuroplasticity*, which has been previously mentioned, describes this process by which a constant remodeling of the brain and spinal cord occurs. This is the process through which uniqueness of perception takes place, as the nervous system is constantly trying to accurately interpret its environment.

During the period of embryonic and fetal growth, neuroplasticity is at its peak. And during the first two years of life, the ability to remodel and change is dramatically enhanced. Subsequently, as we age, this ability gradually declines and is less robust. But even so, neuroplasticity persists to a degree, even through old age. Advances in rehabilitative efforts, biofeedback, and other manipulations of sensory inputs have demonstrated this dynamic ability of the nervous system.

In essence, the three phases of migration and local development, morphogenesis, and adjustment and refinement comprise the key developmental features of the brain. The precise destination and the pathway neurons and nerve fibers travel eventually create an intricate and detailed network involving billions of cells. Through proteins, neurotrophic factors, neurochemicals, and gene regulation, these road maps are followed with great care. And even after successfully reaching their end point, ongoing adjustments and pruning continue to make the system as accurate as possible.

General Organizational Considerations

Now that we have appreciated the complexity of brain and spinal cord development, attempting to comprehend how the brain perceives reality may seem impossible. However, what we have learned about the brain is that the developmental process establishes a very organized and predictable anatomy. Separation of motor and sensory areas is established, as are regional areas tailored to specific functions. By our gaining a grasp of this general organization, understanding the brain's anatomy is made much easier. Before considering individual trees, it's best to get a handle on the overall forest.

First, the nervous system is arranged in a 'down to up' type of organization. The farther down the brain and spinal cord you travel, the more primitive and simple the function becomes. For example, a basic knee reflex travels along nerve pathways from the knee to the lower spinal cord and back to the leg. No higher brain function is involved. Breathing and the rate of a heartbeat are likewise reflexes of the nervous system. Because their control is more vital to an organism, these functions are managed in the brain stem. And even farther up, complex functions such as localizing a moving object, associating an event with an emotion, and even discriminating thought are located in the higher cortex regions of the brain.

As one performs more complex mental functions, the higher levels in the nervous system are used. Similar comparisons can be made between the human brain and the animal brain. Moving from the spinal cord to the brain stem and to the brain, there are progressively few similarities between the human nervous system and various animal nervous systems. Human beings become more unique as higher levels in the nervous system are reached.

While there is a lower-to-higher organization of function within our nervous systems, organization into left and right sides also occurs. In general terms, most of the nerves in the left side of the body connect to the right side of the brain, and most of the nerves in the right side of the body connect with the left side of the brain. Nerves from the body enter the spinal cord and either cross to the opposite side immediately or travel up the spinal cord, crossing over at a higher level. This pattern isn't true for every system, however. For example, both sides of the brain receive hearing from the left side and the right side. Some visual inputs cross to the opposite side, while some stay on the same side. But as a general rule, sensory inputs from one side of the body connect with the opposite side of the brain, and motor outputs from one side of the brain control the opposite side of the body.

In addition to the laterality of sensory inputs and motor outputs, the left and right sides of our brains handle different mental operations as well. The left brain is responsible for symbolic recognition to a much greater extent in most people. This means language, calculations, motor programs, and symbol naming are predominantly left-brain functions. It is the logic side of the brain. In contrast, the right brain tends to be more visuospatial in its operations. Facial recognition, pattern recognition, spatial orientation, and abstract concepts are predominantly right-brain functions in the majority of people. Both sides of the brain have the capacity to perform all functions, but as the brain matures, specialization in each side within these domains becomes more pronounced.

As a starting point, these three general concepts can help one appreciate the organizational structure of the brain. To summarize once again, these are the following:

- From lower levels to higher levels, the nervous system becomes more specialized and complex.
- The majority of sensations and motor functions of the body connect to areas on the opposite side of the brain.
- For most, the left side of the brain handles symbol and language recognition, and the right side handles visual, nonverbal, and spatial concepts.

Now that we have described these basic aspects of brain function, we can discuss more site-specific aspects.

Site-Specific Functions of the Nervous System

Now that we have established a basic level of understanding of the nervous system's organization, further understanding of the brain's functions can now be detailed. This becomes important not only for appreciating the organization of the brain but also for understanding how perception takes place. For these reasons, a description of different brain locations and their responsibilities will be mentioned.

The brain is the part of the central nervous system located above the level of the spinal cord. This includes the brain stem, the cerebellum, and the various lobes of the upper brain on the right and left sides. From the brain stem to the frontal cortex, a progressive increase in complexity and neural integration occurs, which accounts for more advanced functions at higher levels. The following is an overview of each of these regions.

Brain Stem Structures

The brain stem, just above the spinal cord, is relatively primitive compared to the rest of the brain. In evolutionary terms, this region is the oldest. The lower brain stem serves to maintain basic survival functions of the human body. These functions include breathing, heart rate, blood pressure, sleep patterns, and other primitive functions. Like the spinal cord, almost all the activities of the brain stem are below the level of consciousness. But unlike the spinal cord, the brain stem handles more complex reflexes, which are more vital.

In regard to perception, the brain stem serves as a conduit for sensory input. For example, tactile information from the body travels through the brain stem, where it is integrated with other nervous system functions. Suppose you are asleep when an insect bites your leg. The pain and touch sensations from the bite travel to the brain stem, where your level of alertness increases, waking you from sleep. This activity occurs at a brain stem level but is below the level of alert awareness.

The best way to think of the brain stem in terms of perception is to view it as a filtering mechanism, where sensory information is directed to the right areas of the brain. In addition, it identifies urgent sensory signals affecting vital functions and reacts accordingly. In other words, the brain stem is a relay station that gives perceptual information a first-pass glance.

Cerebellum

The cerebellum is likewise a relatively primitive neural structure, which lies behind the brain stem. Its primary function is related to the control of balance and coordination of movements. Walking, running, speech, and other motor functions are finely tuned to yield precise movements, allowing discrete actions. Though not a significant part of direct perceptual systems, the cerebellum serves as a relay system for motor functions.

The cerebellum provides feedback information on how effective planned movements are performed. This feedback allows more accurate movements through a monitoring system, which in turn also helps establish accurate eternal perceptions. If one reaches for a pin and the movement is slightly awry, visual and tactile sensory inputs then help the cerebellum adjust the movement to a greater degree of accuracy. Therefore, the cerebellum performs important functions in the perception of the world by monitoring movements in space.

Limbic Area

Situated above the brain stem, the main part of the brain occupies two distinct sides called the cerebral hemispheres. The different functions of the left and right sides have been described previously to an extent. But within each hemisphere, several regions are present and subspecialized in their function. Of these regions, the limbic area is located closest to the brain stem in proximity. Because of this, it is more primitive compared to other areas of the cerebral hemispheres from an evolutionary perspective. Similarities between the limbic region in human beings and in other mammals are quite significant.

Specifically, the limbic areas of the brain are involved with the perception of emotions, the perception of affect, and the attachment of memories to events and activities. In addition, the limbic region assists in controlling hormonal systems that influence bodily function and survival. The interaction of emotion, memory, and hormonal systems allows instinctual responses that aren't always influenced by thoughtful awareness. However, unlike the brain stem, conscious awareness more commonly influences these response patterns.

For example, a sudden rise in carbon dioxide in the blood stream may trigger the brain stem to suddenly increase the breathing rate. This chemical reflex (located in the brain stem) effectively ventilates the lungs more rapidly, thus reducing carbon dioxide levels back to normal. In contrast, consider a situation that makes a person anxious. Perhaps the situation reminds the person of a prior trauma. The situation, its memory, and its association with trauma trigger an emotional response that increases respirations as part of an adrenaline surge. Though these inputs increase respiratory rate the same way the rise in carbon dioxide did, the interplay is more complex.

Perceptual awareness can influence the limbic system. A person may come to recognize (be conscious of) a situation as being associated with a traumatic event and as promoting anxiety. In this case, conscious control of the instinctual emotional and behavioral response can occur. Recognizing the pattern, a person can learn to avoid the typical emotional response. This is distinctly different from the brain stem reflexes previously described. Higher levels of the nervous system become not only more complex in their perceptual abilities but also more intimately related to conscious awareness.

Higher Cortical Functions of the Brain

The cortex of the brain, which comprises the most highly developed nervous system structures, is responsible for the most complex form of thought and informational processing. Six layers of well-organized neurons are arranged in vertical columns and interconnected by hundreds of thousands of neural networks to other regions of the nervous system. It is within this intricate web that perceptual information about our environment and ourselves is received, processed, and analyzed.

In both left- and right-brain hemispheres, several regions are labeled as lobes. These regions, from back to front, include the occipital lobes, the temporal lobes, the parietal lobes, and the frontal lobes. Characteristic grooves, called "fissures," separate these lobes. Each lobe has unique subspecialized functions. For example, the occipital lobes specialize in visual information while the frontal lobes are involved in motor function and planning. Like the rest of the nervous system, very detailed organization enables these specific processing abilities.

The main functions of the cerebral cortex include perception, planning, and attention. From the back regions of the brain to the front, there is a division of function. The back regions, which include the occipital lobes, the parietal lobes, and part of the temporal lobes, are involved in sensory perception. This means these areas receive sensory input from the environment. Visual, auditory, and tactile information and other sensory information are relayed through the spinal cord, brain stem, and cerebellum to eventually arrive in the posterior cerebral cortex. Here sensory information is analyzed and processed among billions of neurons and thousands of neural networks.

In contrast, the front part of the cerebral cortex, which encompasses the frontal lobes and part of the temporal lobes, has different responsibilities. Its functions are more concerned with output rather than input. Cortical areas in front of our brains are responsible for the movement of our bodies, where we focus our attention, and how we plan our movements and actions. Though different brain regions have specific areas of expertise, the gross organization reveals that the back or posterior brain is organized for sensory information input, and the front anterior brain is organized for motor and attention output.

In the most anterior aspects of our brains, much of our social communications and actions is planned. However, our feelings, the tone of voice we use, our facial expressions, and how we conduct self-observation all originate in the front part of our brains. In a sense, these activities are social outputs as opposed to physical outputs, such as movement.

The cortical regions of the brain house billions of neurons, all of which are interconnected in various ways. Within the six layers of vertical columns of neurons, vertical interconnections exist between upper and lower neurons. Horizontal interconnections among various columns are also present. And massive cortical interconnections occur between the left and right cerebral hemispheres. These networks of interconnections are what allow the brain to compare and contrast information and to refine plans and actions. Continuous feedback is being provided for every cerebral action, enabling as much accuracy as possible. At these levels of higher cortical function, perceptual processing of all environmental inputs occurs. In short, basic perception takes place in the cerebral cortex.

While the brain has a division of labor and subspecialization in different regions, the presence of comprehensive neural networks is what allows information to be processed into a cohesive bundle of perceptual information. Physical data is combined with memories, emotions, and concepts to produce a complex interpretation of our environment and ourselves. Continuously changing connections between axons and dendrites occurs as perceptual information is received and functional output is created. Unlike the basic input and output modes of a computer, the human brain is a constantly changing organ capable of adaptation. It is each brain's ability to adapt and change that indeed creates a uniqueness for each person.

How Basic Perception Works

With a very basic understanding of the brain's anatomy, we can now discuss how perception within the human nervous system takes place. For the purpose of explanation, let's suppose you are traveling along the Pacific Coast Highway at sunset. As you travel along at fifty miles per hour, the setting sun paints brilliant colors over the Pacific Ocean. Simultaneously, curves in the road require your attention, as does oncoming traffic. How is it possible for the brain to grasp all this information and accurately perceive it well?

Let's take one component at a time. Visually the brain has a lot to contend with. Colors of the sun over the water, the colors of the road and the surrounding terrain, and colors of the instrumentation panel of the car are being processed at the same time. Also shapes of images are being collected as are calculations about movements and speed of movements. The human visual system categorizes visual information primarily into color, shape, and motion. Each of these components are processed independently and eventually analyzed together.

The visual image enters through the eye of the retina. Specialized neurons capture the images through various chemical reactions and then pass along impulses to other nerves in the upper brain stem. Images on the right and left sides of the environment are organized into different bundles of nerves. Nerves carrying information about are organized separately from those carrying motion and color information. Ultimately this information travels to the back of the cortex, where temporal, parietal, and occipital lobes process the data. Likewise, thousands of interconnections with memory areas, emotional areas, and primitive brain regions allow more complex perceptions of the images. In the end the entire visual picture of the outside world is recreated within the higher cortical regions of the brain.

Similarly, auditory information and tactile information about a visual scene is channeled to the cortex through various channels of basic sensory input. Like the visual system, this input ascends to higher levels within the brain and becomes enriched as other sensory inputs combine with it to create progressively more complex perceptions. Basic perception thus occurs as a step-by-step process from simple inputs to increasingly more complex representations internally. Ultimately, a complete recreation of our external environment on the Pacific Coast Highway is present within our brains.

There are a couple of important points that need to be made here. First, the ongoing integration of perceptual data within the higher cortical regions isn't a static process. With each millisecond, new sensory input is being received, new memories are being formed, and prior data is being reanalyzed. The perceptual process is in constant flux. And no matter how accurate the recreation of the perceived environment may be, there inherently exists a degree of error. As errors in perception are realized, our brains' perceptual images correct them. But many discrete errors are never corrected due to inaccurate or insufficient sensory input, impaired perceptual abilities, or several other aspects of "normal" dysfunction.

The second point is that our emotions and memories influence our perception of our visual scene. No two people have the same exact experiences and emotions. Even identical twins don't share common experiences despite having identical DNA. If one twin develops a purely genetic disorder, the chance that the other twin will get the disorder as well is very high but not necessarily 100 percent. The environment and experiences within the environment alter genetic expression. Similarly, we each have slightly different perceptions of the world around us.

The constant state of flux and the association with memories and emotions are what create perceptual uniqueness for everyone. Despite a fixed real environment, on which perception is based, the recreation and constant analysis of our external world within our brains prevent an exact error-free replica. Every single one of us has a unique perceptual experience of our environment and our own bodies. This opens the door not only for individuality but also for pathological conditions of perception, such as hallucinations, delusions, and more.

Notably, the detailed process by which nerve impulses, neurochemicals, and feedback system provide complex perceptual assessments hasn't been detailed here. Nor has the challenging aspect of perpetual awareness been discussed. Recreating a nearly exact replica of our external environment is one thing, but how do we actually become aware of the perception's meaning and relevance? How do we jump from basic perception to perceptual awareness and consciousness?

Different perspectives account for different answers to these questions. Unique oneness theory, of course, has its own theorized answers. In the next chapter, an overview of how neural networks function will be provided, and subsequent chapters will attempt to address the more complex issues pertaining to conscious perception. Having a general concept of the brain's anatomy and organization should allow a foundation on which to understand these more tedious considerations.

CHAPTER 5

The Physiology of Perception

Thus far, a bottom-to-top system of function for the brain and nervous system has been described. Features of our outside world stimulate various sensory receivers in our bodies, which in turn transmit information that is then relayed to progressively higher and more complex systems, where neural integration occurs among thousands of neural networks. This information is then packaged so that a replica of the outside environment can be recreated. And with this replication, memories, emotional content, and other higher brain information are added to the perceptual process.

The leap from this basic platform of complex perception to actual perceptual awareness is a large one and one unique oneness theory resolves through its propositions. However, before we consider these larger issues, a better understanding of how our nervous system receives sensory information is important. It wasn't too long ago that the brain was thought to operate only by means of electrical impulses. But the discovery of peptide receptors, ligands, and other intricate cellular components changed how we not only saw neuronal communications but also perceptually understood the development of emotions, feelings, and memories.

In this chapter, an introduction to the world of sensory inputs and neurotransmitters will be described. By no means is this meant to be highly technical or comprehensive. However, by having a general understanding of these concepts, you can understand why some theorists have proposed that perceptual awareness may be completely harnessed within the human brain. Current knowledge of neurophysiology is without a doubt impressive in its scope. But it still cannot bridge the gap between perception and consciousness. To appreciate this dilemma, a foundation of basic neurophysiology will be provided.

Chemical Messengers

Early in the twentieth century, the prevailing opinion of how the brain functioned was defined through electrical means. Electrical impulses traveled from one neuron to another by way of an electrical "action potential." This electrical wave would jump from the axon of one neuron to the dendrite of another the same way a row of dominoes would collapse on each other. Science supported this theory, and the similarities between the brain and electrical machines were easy to compare.

But as time passed, new discoveries led to radically new concepts about neurophysiology. Small proteins located in the cell membrane of neurons were found to receive chemical stimulation from other neurons. And the electrical signals known to exist actually triggered the release of these chemicals between neurons. These chemicals were, in essence, tiny messengers that worked in conjunction with the action potential. They transmitted an electrical signal from one neuron to another. Thus, these chemicals became known as neurotransmitters.

What is the role of these chemicals or neurotransmitters? And what makes up these receptors? Interestingly, though different compounds can act as neurotransmitters, the majority fall into the category of proteins or protein components. Proteins are structures made up of many building blocks, called "amino acids." If a protein has a relatively small number of amino acids, it is called a "polypeptide." If it contains hundred or more amino acids, the term *protein* is more common. Regardless of the nomenclature, most receptors and neurotransmitters are composed of amino acids and proteins. How these proteins function to enhance communications between cells is nothing short of remarkable.

Imagine you work for the CIA. You have critical information that must be taken to headquarters. You arrive at headquarters, but for you to be allowed entry, you must first show proper credentials. Perhaps even a retinal scan is needed. Once your credentials are verified, you are allowed inside, where you make your report, revealing critical information that changes internal operations. Headquarters then decides to take further action. In considering receptors and neurotransmitters, these agents operate much the same way. From identity checks to the processing of information, the pattern is very much the same.

Receptors are typically large proteins located in the cell membrane of the neuron and are responsible for "checking the credentials" of various neurotransmitters. Suppose a neurotransmitter comes into contract with a cell membrane receptor. If the credentials match, the neurotransmitter then "docks" into the receptor, much like one puzzle piece fits into another. Once the neurotransmitter attaches to the receptor, a cascade of events then takes place within the neuron to evoke changes. In other words, the neurotransmitter provides information to the cell by way of the cell receptor and causes changes to occur in the cell. These changes may cause new cell proteins to be manufactured, stimulate the expression of DNA, or result in an electrical action potential that then communicates with another neuron downstream. Simplistically, this is how neurotransmitters and receptors function.

Talking with Neurotransmitters

How do neurotransmitters come into contract with their receptors? Do they simply appear haphazardly, or is there an organized process? Like the rest of the nervous system, a very organized process determines if and when a neurotransmitter appears at the receptors' docking station. Most neurotransmitters are released from the axons of other neurons adjacent to the dendrites of another nerve cell. When an electrical action potential makes its way to the end of an axon, tiny vesicles containing neurotransmitter are released through the cell membrane. These chemicals then migrate outside the neuron across a narrow space called the "synaptic cleft" to reach the dendrite of another neuron. Dendrites, compared to axons, contain a much higher number of receptors. The neurotransmitter then binds to its appropriate receptor and communicates needed information to the next neuron. From here, the process begins again to the next neuron or neurons in the network.

In any given experience, imagine the sheer number of neurons involved. To perceive the words and sentences of this book, you must visually process the text and access language, memory, and other brain areas. Hundreds of nerve cell communications occur every few seconds as you read sentence to sentence. And each communication is conducted through electrical potentials and neurotransmitter chemical communications. Humbling, isn't it? Dozens of neurotransmitters are known to exist with each, causing different patterns of response. And we have just begun to scratch the surface. Many other neurotransmitters undoubtedly exist, which have yet to be identified.

Like receptors, most neurotransmitters are proteins, and groups of neurotransmitters are classified according to their basic structure. Some are amino acids, the smallest building blocks of proteins. Some are called "monoamines" because their protein structure has a single "amine" or ammonia group attached to its structure. And some are labeled "peptides" because they represent larger proteins. Other chemicals also function as neurotransmitters and include steroids, hormones, vitamins, minerals, and more. Knowing the different types of neurotransmitters isn't necessarily important for us to consider the mechanisms of perception. However, this understanding does allow one to appreciate why some experts suspect conscious perception is completely housed within the nervous system. The incredible intricacy of neurotransmitter function makes such a consideration attractive.

You may easily recognize several neurotransmitters identified by name. Dopamine, norepinephrine, epinephrine, and serotonin are some of the more common neurotransmitters, which have been popularized through health talks, pharmaceutical commercials, and other educational venues. Other common ones also include acetylcholine, histamine, adenosine, and glycine. However, you may have never heard of some of the more prevalent neurotransmitters. Every few months, new chemicals are being identified with new properties and effects on cell receptors. And slowly, we keep making progress in understanding how our nervous system perceives the world around us.

Of all the connections or synapses between neurons, 90 percent have the neurotransmitter glutamate present. Glutamate is an amino acid that serves to excite the next neuron when released. For example, if a neural network is involved in perceiving touch, glutamate is released between neurons when the skin is touched, triggering activation of this network and eventually perception of the touch. In contrast 90 percent of all synapses that don't have glutamate present contain a chemical called GABA. GABA, which stands for gamma-aminobutyric acid, is also an amino acid. But unlike glutamate, neurotransmitters inhibit citation of the next neuron. Just as glutamate turns on a neuron, GABA turns it off.

Unfortunately, having neurotransmitters turn on and off different neurons for an effect is much more complex than this. Some neurotransmitters indeed activate or suppress subsequent neuron activity, but many others cause specific changes within the next neuron that range from gene expression to new compound formation. Neurotransmitters are also involved in the changes associated with neuroplasticity. So while these chemical messengers provide immediate information to nerve networks, they also invoke changes to the network structure. Over time networks change, depending on the information neurotransmitters provide, the frequency with which they provide it, and the size of their message.

You may have never known someone who suffered a nerve injury. But if you have, you might have noticed that the size of the muscle associated with that nerve shrinks in size afterward. The absence of the nerve (due to injury) results in an absence of neurotransmitters and other chemicals. And in time the muscle shrinks not only from lack of use but also from lack of nerve stimulation. The same thing happens in the brain and spinal cord. If a neuronal network is no longer active, the neurons of that pathway contract. Their dendrites reduce in number or have fewer receptors, and adjacent neurons become less active as well. The opposite occurs when a neural network is used more commonly. The term "use it or lose" has relevance in this regard. This is the basic process by which neuroplasticity molds brain networks to adjust to environmental changes.

Neurotransmitters therefore speak to other neurons and provide communications in milliseconds that enable perceptions and actions to occur. By having discretely organized neuronal networks, the ability to perceive one stimulus occurs efficiently. And as multiple perceptions occur, their integration into a more complex perception becomes possible through more elaborate neuronal communications in the cortex.

Gateways, Inhibition, and Feedback

One of the common themes in the nervous system, and actually in the body, is the system by which adjustments and refinements occur. As sensory inputs travel from the body up through the nervous system, neurotransmitters and neural networks refine the signal as it reaches progressively more complex levels. Some neural paths are shut down while others are activated, and the combination of paths that are "on" and "off" determines an eventual perception recorded.

For example, perhaps you suddenly are touched with a hot iron and for the moment suppose you are blindfolded. How do you perceive where the iron is touching you? Pain receptors in the skin send information through the nerves and nervous system through the activation of pathways leading to the brain. But while these pathways are stimulated, others must be inhibited or shut off. Nerve pathways or networks that serve adjacent skin areas to where the iron is touching the skin are suppressed. This enables more discrete localization between the affected skin and the unaffected skin. As you quickly jerk the arm away from the hot iron, excitation of some muscles of your arm occurs while other muscles are inhibited. This reciprocal give-and-take is a common pattern of how neural networks function.

The detailed organization with which the nervous system operates is what allows such precision in communications. There is a constant flux of excitation and inhibition, positive and negative, and stimulating and suppressing information being provided. If these inputs are relatively balanced, then an input never reaches higher levels of perception. However, if an input reaches a significant level of excitation, the neuron passes the signal along to the network that eventually created a perception of the event. Whether an input reaches a necessary threshold determines whether the gateway is opened to the next level.

If your skin receives a touch, then the receptors on the skin are directly stimulated, causing nerves in your bodies to carry an electrical signal to the neurons of the spinal cord. Here greater amounts of neurotransmitter are released, which in turn stimulate the next nerve in the neuronal network. The neurotransmitters shift the balance in favor of excitation, the gateway is opened, and the electrical signal continues to travel to the next level of the nervous system. In contrast, if input on the skin is so subtle that it doesn't trigger enough neurotransmitters to be released, then the gateway is never opened. In this instance, the neural pathway is never activated.

Excitation, inhibitions, thresholds, and gateways therefore regulate which neural pathways conduct information and which ones lay dormant. And neurotransmitters lie at the heart of this determination. But another important concept to understand is that of feedback systems. Given our same example of the hot iron, how does the brain perceive that movement of the arm effectively allowed the skin to escape the hot iron? If it didn't, then additional actions would need to be taken. Feedback systems provide direct information back to the nervous system, helping to further refine perception. This allows continual readjustments to occur within our perceptual replica so our environmental perception is as accurate as possible.

Predominantly, feedback systems are inhibitory in nature. If a perceptual experience triggers an action, the effective function of that action to change the perceptual experience inhibits that sensory input. If an action is taken to grasp an object but that action is inaccurate, we adjust our perceptions to refine the movement so a successful action is accomplished. In this way, movements also contribute to our perception of the world. Direct sensory inputs play a large role, but indirect sensory feedbacks are also important. Feedback information about movement accuracy and about whether anticipated events occur in response to actions alters our perceptions significantly.

This complex array of functions within the nervous system is what ultimately determines how we perceive the world around us and our bodies. But unlike robots and computers, we aren't simply a summation of positive and negative inputs. We attach not only memories to our experiences but also emotions and feelings. Artificial intelligence has developed ways in which data can be used to gain complex algorithms of reactions. However, as human beings we also experience feelings about our world and responses. Do emotions also come from the nervous system?

Neurotransmission of Emotion

As mentioned in earlier chapters regarding brain anatomy, certain regions of the brain store emotions and emotional memory. Specifically, the limbic regions of both sides of the brain house various emotions and feelings. These may include emotions of happiness, sadness, fear, surprise, and others. And as perceptual information is processed at higher levels of the nervous system, sensory experiences are linked or associated with different emotions. Likewise, memories of past experiences are often attached to feelings. All this information can be later used to further process perceptual experiences in an ongoing fashion.

The belief that emotions are located within the limbic regions evolved from experiments done in the early twentieth century on epilepsy patients. While the patients were awake and conscious during direct brain tissues stimulation, researchers could evoke a vast array of emotions by electrically stimulating limbic areas. Facial expressions and subjective reports of emotions verified their findings. Therefore, accepting the fact that emotional response and likely emotional memory attachments are housed in the brain offered little debate.

From an evolutionary perspective, base emotions stem from either two categories, pain or pleasure. All emotions fall into one of these two base emotion categories. Thus, when one is hungry, a feeling of anxiety may develop emotionally because there is concern over ultimate survival. This emotion would fall into the category of pain. Alternatively, sexual relationships evoke positive emotions, which naturally stimulate pleasure feelings; whether one feels happy or sad, content or anxious, confident or fearful, emotions fall into a dichotomy of either mostly pleasurable or painful. And as a result, perceptions and reactions are flavored with this information. This then drives one to either avoid pain or seek pleasure, depending on the situation.

In latter parts of the twentieth century, it became increasingly apparent that emotions are affected by not only neural connections but also bodily connections. For example, the release of testosterone from sex organs can stimulate aggressive feelings. Pain in a body part can trigger the release of substances that trigger anxiousness, fear, and/or anger. And circulating chemicals provided through medications can also affect emotions. Opiates are well known to cause not only pain relief but also a feeling of euphoria or happiness. The point is that emotions are perceived ultimately through limbic region networks, but their origins are often elsewhere in the body through neurochemicals transmission.

In Darwin's evolutionary theory, he noted that the same muscles a wolf used when growling were the same ones human beings used when angry. Therefore, despite there being subtle differences in appearance because of anatomical variations, the root of these expressions was housed within neural networks and programmed through evolution. Indeed this information has been repeatedly verified. It appears that emotions indeed have a primary residence within the limbic regions of the brain, as do our emotional memories and responses.

Like other parts of the nervous system, the limbic regions are subject to neuroplasticity as well. Continuous stimulations with sensory input that reveals pain and suffering create chronic emotional changes in an individual. Post-traumatic stress disorder and chronic anxiety states reflect clinical disorders that represent such changes. By the same token, behavioral therapy through providing positive perceptual information can improve such conditions, even in the absence of medication therapy. These responses to changing environmental stimulation support that the limbic regions behave the same way as other components of the nervous system in response to change.

Emotional perception of our environment thus seems to reside within the brain and nervous system. An experience in the world can evoke feelings of anger or happiness, even when we may not be conscious of the exact nature of the events. How many times have you found yourself irritated but didn't necessarily know why? When you think back to your recent experiences, you then recall that someone made a comment that upset you. However, even though you didn't consciously become aware of that emotion, your nervous system still registered the feeling. This perceptual event and its related emotional reaction all occurred at a level below awareness or consciousness. Given what we understand about the limbic system and neurotransmission, this emotional perception indeed occurs within the brain.

Body and Environment

From the discussion so far, you might assume neurotransmitters are located only within the nervous system itself. However, neurotransmitters are also located throughout the body. And as mentioned earlier, many chemicals can serve to stimulate nerve inputs within the body and the brain itself. Hormones and steroids are common chemicals that circulate throughout the entire body and provide perceptual communications between the body and brain.

Much like our outer world, our bodies must be perceived. Just as you would envision a car traveling along the highway, you must also envision your body. The image of your body as fat or thin, the texture of your skin, and the location of a discomfort or sensation are all perceptions the brain must accommodate. What your body looks like in reality is just as complicated as the world itself. And the perceptual system of the brain must create an internal replica of the body within its confines just as it does for the external environment. In this regard, one's body is part of the external world.

This may sound a bit strange, since most of us believe our bodies are actually part of ourselves. And, in fact, they are. But our ability to perceive our bodies is no different from our ability to perceive our world. Just as the perception of our world is unique to us because our brains recreate a perceptual replica of it, the perception of our bodies is likewise unique. Others may perceive your body differently in miniscule degrees than you yourself perceive it. This is what makes your own body's perception unique and special. But at the same time, your body does exist in reality. This real body is the oneness that exists for everyone, including yourself, to perceive.

Understanding this concept allows you to understand how disorders such as anorexia and bulimia develop. Distorted perceptions of one's body image cause reactions that lead to physical problems of the body. This is no different from burning yourself on a stove because you perceive heat as a normal temperature. The brain uses the same types of neurotransmitters, feedback system, and neural networks to process information about the body as it does about the external world.

The body has numerous ways it provides the brain with perceptual inputs. For example, the presence of food in the stomach triggers both visceral nerves and circulatory hormones to communicate messages to the brain that stimulate bowel activity. These inputs let the brain known about the status of the digestive system. Distention of the bladder muscles notifies the brain and nervous system that one needs to void. These perceptual inputs are important for proper functioning of the body, but they are also an important part of how we perceive our physical appearance and health. In short, our bodies and environment are unified as a perceptual whole. Both have perceptual replicas created mentally that allow us to make determinations and assumptions about reality.

Perceptual Awareness

The ability of the brain and nervous system to collect information about our world and physical bodies is an amazing thing. The degree of organization and precision is mind boggling. Within exquisite detail, the informational inputs are received and distributed in a fashion that allows a recreation of our external world within our minds. And the means by which these systems operate is no less than miraculous. The persistent, unrecognized operations among neurotransmitters, hormones, and steroids at any given time seem almost too incredible to measure. It's exactly this impressive amount of information that enables our brains to reproduce perceptual replicas.

Despite the tremendous array of activities present, there is still one problem in reaching what is considered actual awareness or consciousness. Suppose, with all the inputs available to the brain, a nearly exact replica of the environment and body is established as part of the standard perceptual process. Colors, shapes, movements, textures, smells, and a variety of other inputs allow a recreation of a scene, and memories and emotional constructs are added to enhance the perception. All this creates a rich picture that almost precisely mimics reality. But at what point does a person become aware of this perception?

Let's take the example of smelling a rose. The perception of the rose, the act of smelling it, the fragrance the flower evokes, and the thorns along its stem can all be directly perceived by the brain. Likewise, the pleasant feelings from the fragrance and its beauty can be appreciated mechanically. Even memories that warn of the thorns' potential pain enhance the perception further. But no matter how rich these informational inputs and how complex the brain's interpretation of these inputs are, the ability to step back from this scene and be conscious of its meaning is beyond mechanical perception.

Perceptual awareness or consciousness implies the ability to behold the entire perception and apply it to a higher meaning. Some philosophers have termed this the difference between the brain and the mind. If the brain represents the basic operations of the nervous system that allow perceptual replication of reality, then the mind represents an awareness of the brain's activity in this capacity. Therefore, to be aware of another entity, one must exist outside of it. The brain cannot perceive and be conscious of its own existence and operation simultaneously.

Though the comparison may be stale and simplified, our current day makes it irresistible to compare the brain to a high-level computer. No matter how complex a computer becomes with software programs and greater dynamic memory capabilities, the computer cannot actually become aware of its own presence. Even with the development of artificial intelligence, which involves intricate comparisons and conceptualizations of data sets, the machine is still limited in perceiving its own presence and significance. To truly be conscious of an entity, one must exist outside of the entity.

Even with a near-perfect replica of the external world created in the brain, this replica cannot be consciously perceived without another force outside the brain to recognize it and appreciate its inherent meaning.

Not all neurobiologists and scientists agree with this form of thinking. Their theories hold that interactions among highly complex systems within the brain can actually generate a perceptual capability within the brain itself. This ability, however, has never been demonstrated within the world of science or physics. This doesn't make it necessarily impossible, but many other possibilities could explain this phenomenon, which science refuses to consider.

Science supports a universal approach to life consciousness and perception. In this, everything must fall within the laws of nature and physics that have been defined as valid and true. Anything that cannot be explained through these laws must therefore be invalid or at least seriously questioned. However, one truth doesn't necessarily extinguish the possibility of other truths. Likewise, one truth doesn't have to permeate everything universally to exist. Truths can exist side by side without intermingling. Perhaps the laws of nature and physics might coexist with other laws yet to be identified.

These are the dilemmas when considering perception and perceptual awareness. Science has defined a great deal about perception as it pertains to the nervous system. The characteristics of the basic perceptual systems outlined in this chapter are quite profound, and it's humbling to consider the depths with which our brains recreate our perception of reality. But at the same time, science has come up against obstacles in explaining how such a mechanistic system can explain nonmechanistic concepts such as consciousness and awareness.

In the subsequent chapter, we will define these obstacles and explain why areas such as quantum physics struggle when attempting to define perceptual awareness through mechanistic formulas. By defining these inherent difficulties, we will be able to consider other possibilities to explain how true perception occurs and how unique oneness theory proposes some alternative considerations. These possibilities offer exciting and fresh opportunities to understand human functioning as they pertain to health, and they provide great potential in rendering care to many who suffer existing psychological problems.

CHAPTER 6

Science and Religion Explained

The difficulty of defining consciousness from a purely scientific perceptive has plagued scientists and researchers throughout time. The objective nature of science and the laws of nature demand proof and factual evidence to support hypotheses and theory. Through scientific method, reproducible results have led to incredible discoveries. This act has occurred to such an extent that scientific theories regarding medicine, consciousness, and even the origin of life hold significant credence within society. Yet despite this fact, many shortcomings and deficits still exist in trying to explain perceptual consciousness.

In the preceding chapters, both philosophical theories and scientific knowledge have been presented to demonstrate some basic differences between their approaches. In this chapter, these areas will be explored a bit deeper. But instead of viewing science and philosophy regarding consciousness as conflicting, you are invited to consider how these two areas of study may be in fact one.

Scientific facts and theories don't need to exclude philosophical considerations. When Copernicus stated his heliocentric view of the solar system, the Catholic Church and many religious scholars of his day opposed him. Some viewed him as demonic and atheistic. Eventually his theory of a sun-centered galaxy system proved to be accurate, and religious doctrine incorporated these new facts into its beliefs. Similarly, perhaps it's time for science to open its mind to consider other theories in areas concerning consciousness and perceptual awareness.

The basic problem is that science has been unsuccessful in explaining consciousness, because consciousness isn't amenable for traditional means to measure and quantify it. Not only is consciousness subjective on the part of the individual, but its lack of nonobjectivity makes scientific means unable to truly define it. One can postulate that a variety of electrical and chemical reactions in the brain and nervous system allow an accurate perception of reality, but what about the actual experience that occurs with that perception? A perception can include feelings, emotions, memories, and a variety of sensory information. But the actual experience and awareness of that perception in total is difficult to quantify in scientific terms.

To understand this better, a variety of concepts within scientific theory and its shortcomings will be described. From classical physics to quantum physics and beyond, the challenges science has experienced in explaining the elusive concept of consciousness will be discussed. And within these shortcomings, other possibilities will be offered for further thought. A paradigm shift is needed to gain a greater appreciation of how conscious perception actually takes place and to begin to apply these methods to valid study.

Science and Religion

The differences between science and religion have in themselves been in evolution over time. Both within a single individual and humanity, there exists a constant relationship between these two fields. Interestingly, it was one of the world's foremost scientists and mathematicians who gave a concise description of how religion and science interact. Albert Einstein perhaps described this evolution as well as anyone.

According to Einstein, religion evolved through three different levels. These included religion of primitive man, moral religion, and a final higher level of religious thought. Each of these represented progressively more advanced levels of conceptualization. And with this evolution, science and religion came together. Instead of science and its grounded stance in factual data conflicting with religion's subjective beliefs of the origin of life and consciousness, higher levels of religious understanding and science accommodated each other.

Einstein described that religion about God and ultimate consciousness as evolving from religion of fear at a primitive level. Fear of hunger, illness, and death encouraged the conceptualization of a God who could protect mankind from these fears. Religious priests then served a role to play as mediators between mankind and deity, developing hegemonies by which people would behave. As mankind evolved, along with scientific advances, primitive religions gave way to moral religions.

In contrast to primitive religion, moral religion is less concerned with fears and more concerned with beliefs about rewards and punishments, justice, and the basic ethical values of goodness. In defining a moral religion, God is still defined in man's image, and beliefs are rigidly held that account for wrong and right. Science and moral religions often clash as the rigid beliefs of moral religion conflict at times with objective scientific fact. The previous example of Copernicus is a classic example of this conflict. Even today, much of human society operates within this mode of religion.

Einstein, however, also described a third and higher level of religious experience that goes beyond the moral aspects of religion.

The desire to view the universe as a whole and to rise above human limitations drives the ability to seek a higher religious experience. No longer is God seen as a specific entity in humanlike form, but instead he permeates everything and unifies all. Third-level religious experiences invite creativity and abstract concepts, which no longer divide thought but instead unify it. At this level, truth bridges the gap between science and religion.

These views of Einstein are interesting in that he believed the creativity needed to establish scientific theory and invoke passion for inquiries into the workings of the universe stemmed from a unity between the objective and the subjective. In other words, science alone couldn't explain the universe by objective facts. It needed the subjective creative force and ability to abstractly conceptualize it to postulate theories to examine. Likewise, religion in its highest form accommodated scientific fact into its beliefs.

According to Einstein, the purpose of art and science was to generate an ability to think and experience everything as completely as possible. These fields of study weren't meant to exclude religion and spirituality but instead to advance it. Despite current scientific views to the contrary, Einstein was one scientist who didn't necessarily feel all of existence could be explained through the laws of science and mathematics. Regardless, the advances science has provided have made this mode of thinking more the exception rather than the rule.

Classical Physical and Quantum Mechanics

Classical physics dates back to at least the time of Isaac Newton. Newton's mathematical equations that defined how matter behaves in gravitational fields established an example by which laws of nature were determined with seemingly exact precision. These deterministic theories and laws led to a division between science and religion or science and philosophy. If nature behaved according to exact laws, how could an outside entity influence their behavior? Did God even truly exist, or could everything be explained through science alone?

As classical physics progressed, different types of force interactions were defined. They included not only gravitational forces but also strong forces, weak forces, and electromagnetic forces. The more science explained the behavior of matter within the universe, the less it appeared that divine influence may exist. The single path of an atom under known conditions could be determined mathematically before the experiment began simply by understanding the known laws of physics.

Darwinian theories took this a step further, imposing a hypothesis of how the creation and evolution of matter came to exist. Though the intricacies of nature and physics were far from being understood, Darwin made remarkable discoveries, demonstrating within species how survival of the fittest determined how one animal or plant may be naturally selected over another. Those entities in nature equipped to best survive would naturally be propagated, allowing a stronger species to evolve. Eventually, this would lead to adaptation of an entirely new species if natural environments demanded this.

Science was beginning to show that everything could actually be determined through mechanisms and laws that governed all matter and nature. The goal of science was simply to figure out these laws, which in turn would unlock the secrets to the universe. These discoveries and theories affected all fields of science and life. Medicine, physics, chemistry, and physiology adopted this deterministic perspective, as did other areas of civilized society, including education, art, and even some religions. Indeed, everything appeared to be within the scope of classical physics and its inherent logical concepts.

Despite its accomplishments, classical physics had several shortcomings. The measurements and calculations believed to explain all the matter fell short when trying to explain moralities, ethics, and individual personalities. The workings of the mind under scientific theories support an array of electrochemical interactions that eventually result in function and behavior. But how do these processes and equations explain free will or ethical beliefs? How do these processes account for the conscious experience of an event?

Albert Einstein's theory of relativity took science a step further. The famous equation $E=mc^2$, which explained how matter and energy could be translated into the other, not only advanced classical physics but also opened the door for quantum physics. The theory of relativity demonstrated that space and time were geometrically related through mathematical determination. If this was the case, then time had to be a continuum just like space. In other words, past, present, and future all existed as a single entity along a continuum the same way the earth and the universe coexist along a continuum in space. The observation that an event is in the past or in the present is simply an illusion of the observer.

The interpretations the theory of relativity made in relationship to space and time raised questions about the observer in relation to classical physics. The deterministic ability to define the activity of matter and energy as well as space and time began to be somewhat obscure. If all these things could be mathematically defined based on scientific theory and if the observer were an integral part of scientific theory, then how could the illusion of past, present, and future be part of this rigid deterministic system? Additionally, how could the laws of physics be used to explain complex systems that had an almost-infinite number of particle paths that were constantly changing?

Quantum physics was science's answer. Where classical physics defined single paths of particles, quantum physics sought to define a complex system of particles and their interactions. This was an attempt to explain facets of the known world that included chance, free will, and illusion. Instead of being a rigid deterministic science, quantum physics was also a nondeterministic field of study. It sought to explain how a system changed over time using traditional laws of physics while simultaneously invoking a degree of chance and unpredictability into the system. This second component, called the "quantum jump" or "collapse of a particle's wave function," was a significant change in a system resulting from causeless chance. In other words, deterministic features were combined with nondeterministic features.

Both the deterministic and nondeterministic components quantum physics suggested were mechanistic processes. Science simply needed to include in its theories of physics a randomness to account for chaos known to occur in complex systems. In theory, if all the conditions in a system within any given moment were known, the complex state of the system could be known. But the problem was that the system was constantly changing, and an infinite number of possibilities could evolve at any particular moment. Particles of matter had to be defined as both particles and waves to accommodate this infinite continuum of space and time. Defining a system seemed to be beyond reach.

While quantum mechanics certainly allowed greater flexibility in defining a system and tried to explain the world more accurately, the introduction of randomness and chance made physics appear much less mechanistic by incorporating nondeterministic aspects. Trying to account for the illusion of time, the impression of an observer and chaos within a system created some difficulties within quantum physics. It seemed that classical physics was trying to place a square peg into a round hole of reality, and the resulting answer was quantum physics.

Despite its complex theories and explanations, and its limitations in explaining the behavior of particles in a system, quantum physics is widely held as a valid explanation of our world today among the scientific community. It is routinely taught at all levels of education and has received little challenge from the mainstream. But perhaps it's time to consider not only mechanistic theories but also nonmechanistic theories of how complex systems behave. Perhaps these considerations could not only explain how particles behave in a chaotic environment but also offer insight into how consciousness, awareness, and perception interact.

Mechanistic and Nonmechanistic Theories

The term *mechanistic* refers to how current-day scientists explain our world. It refers to modern theories of physics, measurements, calculations, and even the origins of life. In mechanistic terms, everything is composed of matter, and matter is fully represented by numbers, mathematics, and the laws of nature. Within this perspective, nothing exists outside a mechanistic domain. Even if something cannot yet be explained, the reason for this is simply that science has yet to find the underlying answer.

By mechanistic philosophies, the workings of the human mind are nothing more than a combination of biochemical processes that begin at basic neural operations and gradually proceed to higher and more complex operations until thoughts, feelings, and perceptions occur. At some level of highly complex mechanistic operation, all human functioning can be explained as can the entire actions and reactions within the universe. With the big bang theory, even the origin of life can be explained through mechanistic concepts. These principles are the foundations of modern-day science.

The effects of Newtonian physics, Darwinism, and quantum physics were to progressively attempt to explain our world and ourselves through the laws of nature. In the process, theories of religion and spirituality fell by the wayside and were touted as being simply mythologies trying to temporarily explain what science would one day reveal. But to date there have been some problems in accepting this over-encompassing view that everything is indeed mechanistic.

For example, Darwinism has never been factually proved to the extent that one species actually evolved into another completely different species. Scientists state this is true only because not enough time has been allowed to pass. But at the rate currently estimated for such an evolution to occur, the ability of one species to evolve into another would take longer than the present estimated age of the earth. Evolutionary theory hardly seems feasible in explaining life in totality.

While mechanistic science defines many everyday laws of physic by which the world operates, it also falls short in explaining issues such as social values, ethics, and morals. If Darwin's theory is taken at face value, survival of the fittest would actually take advantage of these "soft" characteristics unique to human beings. How can such benevolent aspects of human personality be explained as a means of evolution?

Some scientists state that social values are simply a higher-order strategy for survival. In other words, through social moral behaviors, individuals can gain power, safety, and other supports that favor survival. But for those individuals who pay little attention to such values in society, their survival seems unaffected overall. As society has become more civilized, quality and not quantity of life is affected through most judicial processes. In essence, evolutionary theory is very limited when it comes to explaining issues of species origins. And science itself falls short in explaining individual experience, free will, and morality.

So how has society dealt with explaining these areas when science's shortcomings are evident? Throughout history when mechanistic theories have been unable to define logical causes with which to explain phenomena, nonmechanistic theories have been used. Nonmechanistic theories are various religions and spiritualistic beliefs that seek to give purpose to life and explain its meaning. At the same time, nonmechanistic theories offer a possible way to explain consciousness and awareness. Contrary to common thought, mechanistic and nonmechanistic theories can coexist.

Not only cultures and religious scholars but also scientists and philosophers have devised nonmechanistic theories. In general, there have been three categories of nonmechanistic theory that attempt to explain consciousness. These include identity theories, panpsychism, and psychophysical parallelism. Despite their complex names, the underlying beliefs about how consciousness and our physical minds interact are fairly straightforward.

Identity theories basically believe that both conscious experiences and physical actions are real. Because they lend credence to consciousness as a separate concept, this is considered a nonmechanistic theory. However, identity theory supports the idea that consciousness comes from mental events ultimately tied to neural events. In other words, mental and neural phenomena are one and the same. The bottom line is that both can be considered physical happenings, and thus identity theories aren't significantly different from scientific mechanistic theories.

Panpsychism, on the other hand, is more nonmechanistic in its approach. Under the scope of these theories, single unified substance is felt to exist that has dual properties of both the physical and nonphysical. In other words, this substance has the ability to experience consciousness as well as physical events and have an innate sentient aspect. All physical objects thus have the ability to feel or experience some level of sentient experience, whether human or otherwise.

Lastly, psychophysical parallelism also holds that both conscious feeling and physical phenomena are real. Instead of being single, unified substances, both consciousness and physical forms occupy separate entities that are interrelated in a one-to-one fashion. This doesn't indicate that a causal relationship between the two needs to exist. However, this does seek to explain why some events would adhere to laws of nature and others wouldn't. Psychophysical parallelism supports the existence of an entity that allows consciousness and subjective perception that is extraphysical in nature.

While religions have supported a nonphysical entity in the form of God to provide explanations for life, consciousness, and awareness, it is noteworthy to understand that some scientists have also proposed such possibilities. The inability of mechanistic theories to explain many aspects of human life and experience has led to these postulations. Even as mechanistic theories have added nondeterministic components to their deterministic hypotheses to account for chaotic occurrences and randomness, shortcomings still exist. These have left some scientists unsatisfied with mechanistic explanations.

Consciousness and the Computer

With the technological advances of the last several decades, the comparison between the human brain and the computer is inevitable. As more and more has been learned about the electrochemical processes of the brain, analogies to a computer's processors, memory storage, abilities, and computational programs help support mechanistic concepts about how a computer may one day experience its own consciousness. In other words, a computer may eventually be sentient.

Indeed, researchers who work in the fields of artificial intelligence suggest this is possible. By creating hierarchies of programs within the computer, increasingly more complex operations could be performed that would equate to thoughts, feelings, and perceptions. But can a computer really be aware of itself and its surroundings? Could it one day experience reality for itself?

A computer essentially consists of hardware that comprises its central processor unit (CPU), memory storage, and other related components that allow it to carry out mathematical operations. Input data are provided to the computer, and various operations are conducted after being retrieved from memory. Eventually, output data is recorded and/or reported. Through sequential or parallel operations, the computer performs a limited set of instructions at any given time as it relates to its operations. Therefore, how can a computer be aware of these operations at the same moment?

Workers in artificial intelligence believe the answer comes from higher-level computer programs. Above simple arithmetic operations, another level of programs could analyze the results of these functions in a more global manner. And above this level, other programs could obtain an even bigger gestalt of what is occurring. As levels become more complex and removed from the basic operations, symbolic representations are used and begin to create the equivalent of thoughts, feelings, and perceptions. At some level, the creation of "self" is attained.

Unfortunately, this hierarchy of programs has limitations. Even at the level of self, how is the computer aware of the thoughts and feelings defined by its higher-level programs? Higher-order programs might allow the ability to link an operation to a defined emotion, such as sadness, but the computer is still unable to truly experience sadness. It is simply identifying that a complex set of operations yielded a result that fits into a hierarchy classification associated with sadness. This sadness has been defined. But no matter how detailed, complex, or evolved the computer's infrastructure is, it still cannot have an innate awareness of what sadness means or experience sadness subjectively.

To some extent, the brain can be viewed the same way. As lower-order neurons provide sensory information for perception, progressively higher-level neurons and neural networks create communications that allow patterns to be recognized. These are tied to areas of the brain's memory storage, emotional centers, and more to create a complex pattern of behavior. Eventually, this behavior defines the ego of that person. But from there the explanation ceases to provide reasonable answers. The experience and awareness of the thoughts, emotions, and perceptions are possible only if something outside the ego is able to give it subjective (not objective) meaning.

Gerald Edelman has specifically addressed the comparisons between human consciousness and the computational abilities of computers. In his view, computers are unable to achieve the same degree of functioning as the human brain because of their inherent mode of operation. For input to be received, computers must invoke a great deal of decoding and have information presented to them in specific ways. This isn't possible within reality's environment for the brain. Inputs aren't prepared for the brain to receive them in any particularly format. Additionally, computers must have defined operations for every instance of input to function properly, even when input is constantly changing. To have a vast array of responses and operations to meet all the encountered input from the world, the degree of complexity and memory storage would far exceed a computer's capability.

Despite this, Edelman does believe in the ability of the human mind to reach consciousness through higher levels of conceptualization. As neural inputs are channeled through higher-order neurons, programmed responses are selected based on which neural networks are activated or suppressed. Ultimately, these responses lead to more abstract concepts where emotions and thoughts are integrated. If some networks or channels are activated more frequently than others, these pathways become more dominant. This process of plasticity explains learning and adaptability.

Edelman believes in Darwinism as it applies to the brain, and he rejects dualism instead, believing that all mental experiences can be explained through laws of matter. His hierarchy of conceptualization and beliefs of adaptability are the foundations by which he holds these beliefs. But unfortunately, the same problem arises. How can a perceptual experience be conscious and have meaning when the observer and the subject are one and the same? Even if high-level brain functions create a perception rich in emotional, sensory, and logical information, how can it also step back and provide an encompassing meaning to the entire experience? Even though Edelman's thoughts about human consciousness may not have all the answers, he makes logical explanations why the human mind cannot be analogous to the computer.

Implicate Order

One of the more interesting ways by which scientific means is exploring oneness is under the term "implicate order." Physicist David Bohm of Syracuse University has been conducting experiments that support the universality of matter. Quantum physics states that to accurately define all parts of a system, all the variable of that system must be known. With implicate order, Bohm supports that indeed this is possible because everything is one.

In Bohm's experiments, he suspended a drop of ink between two cylinders in a viscous fluid medium composed of glycerin. As one cylinder is rotated, the drop of ink gradually thins into a linear array of ink and eventually disappears. However, if the cylinder is reversed, the stretched ink drop slowly returns to its original form. From this Bohm holds that what appears disorganized is very well organized. The stretched drop of ink becomes unrecognizable as even being composed of ink; but from this condition, it retains its original organized structure, allowing it to return to its droplet form once the cylinder is reversed.

Bohm's terminology for this enfolding and unfolding of matter is "implicate order." His view sees the world and in fact the entire universe as having an implicate order that is enfolded throughout the entire medium. And as things happen, things become unfolded and observable. Therefore, what appears as chaos isn't really chaotic at all. Instead it is enfolded and just waiting to be unfolded. By having everything known and in some type of order, all the parameters of the system are known and allow the laws of quantum physics to apply.

The other notable revelation from this perspective includes that every event, action, and piece of matter is related to another. In other words, there is an absolute oneness existing between all things. Each part contains the whole because one cannot exist without the other. Eliminating any part of the implicate order would thus unravel its entirety.

While Bohm doesn't necessarily support a nonmechanistic origin of this oneness, he does admit that the idea that creates such an implicate order is beyond what can be manifestly known. In addition, the fatalistic aspects of implicate order, with everything being known and simply waiting to play itself out, leave little room for free will. A missing link still exists. There is still a component that fails to account for the origin of oneness, ethical behaviors, free will, and conscious awareness. Implicate order goes a long way to explain how all matter, space, and time may represent a continuum, but it still has a void that can explain nonphysical events.

Trying to Make Sense of It All

By highlighting classical physics, quantum physics, and their limitations in explaining consciousness, the purpose is to create an openness to accepting alternative forms of opinion. Mechanistic theories that seek to define all life through mathematical formulations and laws of physics continue to fall short of their goals. They have added nondeterministic postulations to deterministic laws to try to account for unexplained aspects of the universe, but still these don't explain fundamental aspects about the creation and meaning of life or the presence of conscious awareness.

This doesn't imply by any means that science and its objective discoveries aren't valid. The implication is simply to raise awareness that mechanistic theories may forever fall short if other nonmechanistic systems exist. If another realm of laws coexisted along with the laws of nature, neither would be null and void. Instead, both would be valid and real. But without considering the other set of laws, only part of the answers to reality and consciousness would be possible.

Theories such as the implicate order theory David Bohm proposed provide further evidence that quantum physics and classical physics are indeed valid and likewise may be consistent with a universality and oneness of the universe. But even at this level of explaining the laws of matter, areas outside of matter are needed to explain creation of this order and other humanistic characteristics. Why can't nonmechanistic and mechanistic theories coexist? As Einstein suggested, science, art, and higher levels of religion can all combine to reach a greater understanding of the universe.

In the subsequent chapter, the theory of unique oneness will be discussed in detail. Having laid the foundation for its central concepts, features of both individuality and universality will be highlighted. Just as science and religion can coexist, so can uniqueness and oneness. It's at this level of understanding that opportunities to incorporate mechanistic and nonmechanistic theories are possible. And by allowing this to occur, new ways to understand consciousness and perception can evolve, thus influencing all areas of human life.

CHAPTER 7

Concepts of Unique Oneness Theory

A t this point, we have covered a vast topic area and laid the groundwork by which unique oneness theory can be properly explained. Consciousness has been considered from various philosophical perspectives. Reality and perception likewise have been investigated from different points of view. And in defining what these areas may and may not represent, additional subjects of self and ego have been discussed. All these are relevant to what will now be covered in unique oneness theory.

Currently, there appears to be a relative dichotomy between science and religion. This isn't simply on the basis of separating church and state in a political sense, but its more ingrained in a philosophical sense. Science deals specifically with what is objectively known and what can be measured. It pays attention to things that are reproducible under consistent parameters. As a result, science holds that everything can ultimately be explained by rigid laws that explain the universe. And when these laws fail to explain a known phenomenon, science holds the reason is because the answer has yet to be found.

Religion, on the other hand, bases much of its beliefs on faith. While objective evidence can certainly add to subjective belief systems, they aren't necessarily required for many spiritual or religious considerations. On occasion, however, religious beliefs are so strongly held that they refute clear evidence to the contrary. This push and pull between science and religion has always existed, and as of yet, the two haven't come together as one. Today, evolution theory, quantum physics, and advances in our knowledge of the brain and body have caused the pendulum to swing more toward the side of science. But this doesn't mean science has found all the answers. In fact, science is far from that.

The more we discover about our existence, the more complex the universe seems to become. Classical physics held fairly simple laws of nature, making the world seem explainable according to the properties of matter. But as knowledge about time and space continuums and the theory of relatively were realized, classical systems failed. Quantum physics took its place. But as we have discussed, current laws of physics have many shortcomings as well. So where do we go from here? How do science and religion resolve their differences?

Perhaps Einstein had it correct. Maybe at the most advanced level, science and religion come together and advance humanity's understanding of the universe and beyond. This would, of course, require that science and religion be less rigid in their beliefs and philosophies. Science would need to consider the possibility of things being less objective, at least in theory, and religion would have to accept that faith beliefs are persistently subject to new information. This is the territory where unique oneness theory exists.

The ramifications of a new perspective of looking at reality and our perception of reality extend to all areas of life. One of the most important areas is how we view health. This refers not only to the health of ourselves but even to the health of the planet. In the sections to follow, an explanation of unique oneness theory will be given along with the potential advances that might occur with a new understanding. Greater advances in human history have always been preceded by innovative perspectives that open our minds to new ways of thinking. Hopefully, unique oneness theory can help move us in that direction.

Unique Oneness Theory and Reality

Like other existing philosophies that have been mentioned, unique oneness theory proposes a monistic philosophy. Monism holds that all of reality is one. At an absolute level, everything is part of an organic unity that is inseparable. All the seemingly individual parts are an integral part of the whole. No matter what is perceived, the foundation of perception is real, and the same is true for all of us. This in essence is the oneness to which unique oneness theory ascribes.

From a religious standpoint, this view isn't difficult to conceive. All major religions today including Christianity, Judaism, Islam, Buddhism, and others believe in a central unifying monistic deity or spirit. However, the problem is often the details. While one religion may believe a unifying spirit may permeate everything, others believe only humans may possess such a central spirit. In the latter case, the unifying characteristic among all of reality is through monistic creation. Both viewpoints adhere to monism, but discrete beliefs distinguish the extent to which the spiritual interacts with the material.

From a scientific standpoint, the perspective is more problematic. In a very basic sense, science must believe in an ultimate reality because everything is supported through objective observations. If reality isn't true, then scientific discoveries are inherently flawed.

Science thus believes in a monistic view of the world as well and assumes a true reality exists.

Unfortunately, science has struggled with this reality at times. When quantum physics and quantum mechanics fail to account for randomness and the infinite possibilities of a system's outcome, one of the postulations has been that multiple universes exist. Therefore, our reality was just one of an infinite number of realities, and every moment another infinite number of universes are occurring as system variables change. This scientific attempt to explain reality through quantum physics dilemmas hardly seems monistic.

While neither religion nor science has all the answers, it seems intuitive that reality exists. And for multiple forms of matter and nonmatter to interact on a consistent basis, a unification of all realities must be present to have consistency. Without a consistent uniform reality, the laws of nature wouldn't be reproducible. Mathematical equations wouldn't consistently define behaviors among particles and matters. For this reason alone, one ultimate reality must exist.

Alternative theories suggest that more than one reality may exist. For example, some philosophies suggest an external reality and an internal reality. Both are considered real and valid, but they aren't necessarily the same reality. The production of a perception based on an external reality creates a second internal reality. This internal reality then becomes part of ultimate reality as well. This isn't the view by which unique oneness theory views internal and external realities. As will be explained when considering perception, unique oneness theory believes only one reality, the external reality, truly exists.

The descriptions of implicate order in the preceding chapter highlight how one reality would actually be supported through scientific study. The enfolding and unfolding of a single organic reality are simply the expression of this reality in space and time. At any single point, everything is one. An implicate order exists in the universe, and as a result, every component of the universe relates to the other. Because everything is accounted for within the implicate order, the system (or universe) couldn't exist without any of its parts. At least from the perspective of matter, science is beginning to define how a real oneness could exist.

While internal perceptions of reality may differ from external reality itself, unique oneness theory ultimately believes that only one reality exists. Therefore, it can only be assumed that science and religion must come together eventually in this one reality. One reality means one truth, and for both science and religion to reach their same goals of exposing truth, both must make concessions to arrive at the same destination.

Unique Oneness Theory and Perception

If the view of reality in unique oneness theory represents the oneness, its view of perception best epitomizes its view of uniqueness. However, the two concepts are intimately related. After we explain in considerable detail how the human nervous system operates, the intricate complexity of sensory systems and hierarchical neural networks is apparent. From a mechanical standpoint, this "hardware" allows external reality to be perceived in some form so we can react and respond to it. As information about our world and universe reaches higher levels of our nervous system, more detailed perceptions form. And through experience and refinement, a better internal reality is created.

According to unique oneness theory, internal perception of external reality is unique to each of us. Not only do we have subtle differences in the makeup of our nervous systems, but likewise the continual set of sensory information we receive through experience and observation is distinctive for each person. Therefore, despite external reality being uniform and unified, internal perceptions of this reality are exclusively unique for each individual.

Consider the following example. Two people stand at the edge of a beach. The sun sets in the distance over the ocean. Moment by moment, both individuals visually perceive the setting sun along with all the colors portrayed over the water. Each perceives the smell of the ocean and the fragrances of the plants around the beach. Each feels the breeze blowing gently on his or her face. Reality provides the same stimuli for perception to occur.

But the two individuals are different and unique. One stands slightly north compared to the other, resulting in a slight difference in how the visual stimuli strike the retina. The breeze blows at a slightly different angle for each. The list of slight external variations for the two people watching the sun set seems endless. And this doesn't even take into account their individual past experiences, thoughts, and emotions, which will further flavor the perception as the information arrives to the brain.

Despite the uniqueness of these perceptions, the reality of the sun setting over the ocean is true. It does exist, and it's the same for both people. But any change in the information as it reaches perception can account for different experiences of this same reality. And in time, constant refinement and revisions to perceptual knowledge are being made. In this fashion, the range of subtle variations of perception acceptable within society can be explained as can gross distortions of reality, which occur with hallucinations and delusions.

Neurosciences have gone a great way in helping us understand how the nervous system conveys information to our brains and how that information is received and integrated. Through this knowledge, appreciating the subtle differences in perception can be realized, and neural plasticity can be accepted. It is this precise uniqueness that accounts for individuality despite all of us existing within one organic unity.

Unique Oneness Theory and Consciousness

As has been highlighted in earlier chapters, science has come a long way in explaining the behavior of matter. But by accepting physics, evolution, and implicate order at face value, science still doesn't come close to explaining how the awareness and experience of perceptions occur. We have described the unique aspect of perceptual abilities of an individual and the oneness of reality, but what does unique oneness theory hold in regard to consciousness?

Consciousness as an entity refers to an innate awareness that exists separate from perception. While perception can depict a near-exact replica of reality within each of us, the ability to appreciate this perception as an observer requires a separate form. Some scientists believe that at higher levels of neural complexity, abstraction and symbolic patterns allow some kind of self-awareness, but unique oneness theory believes this to be impossible.

Even if highly complex patterns of perception were able to make some sense of lower-level information, how could these patterns be aware of their own highly complex operations simultaneously? This would still require another observer. This has been termed 'the little man in the head' problem. In other words, as man perceives his world around him, another "little man" is then required to be aware of the perception as an external observer. Current theories in science cannot justifiably account for this problem.

In addition, other questions are raised about how higher complex patterns of mental activity could support the development of morality and ethics. When some ethical behavior is clearly against self-survival, why would a mental awareness based on evolutionary and neuroscientific patterns ever decide to act morally and not in its self-interest? These shortcomings remain present despite the recent progress in science over the last several decades.

Unique oneness theory holds that it's not only possible but also likely that a nonmaterial entity exists and is integrally related to matter and the universe. This isn't unlike some of the Eastern religious philosophies discussed earlier in the book. In some philosophies, the soul, matter, and God represent real entities, and these entities are all united through organic relationships. This principle of organic relation is supported by unique oneness theory, but this isn't simply based on philosophies alone. In fact, objective evidence of this relationship is being demonstrated.

Consciousness in theory is felt to reflect a separate but related entity that interacts with mental activity. This provides the awareness of reality through an interpretation of perceptions and accounts for our individual and collective experiences. For some religions, this may be referred to as the soul. And the soul uses the tools of the body and mind to function in reality. This nonmaterial life source is the observer that uses the body and mind to gain information about the world around us and in turn interpret its meanings.

For scientists, this consideration may be absurd because the presence of a completely separate entity that doesn't abide by the laws of nature cannot be clearly demonstrated at present. However, some scientific studies have supported its existence, as will be highlighted. Why couldn't another entity that operates by a different set of rules interact with matter? Matter would still have to operate within its system, but that doesn't preclude the existence of something entirely different.

Until the early nineteenth century, infrared light wasn't known. With the use of a prism and a thermometer, William Herschel could detect the presence of infrared light below the light frequency of the color red. Because our visual system couldn't perceive it, infrared light was nonexistent prior to this discovery. Perhaps the same applies to an entire system of nonmaterial realities. Because we keep trying to see them through a lens of physics and mathematics, they appear not to exist. Maybe the time has come to establish means by which such a system could be better observed.

Universal Reciprocity

By unique oneness, the concept of universal reciprocity is highlighted as a key component of this theory. Universal reciprocity refers to the fact that at every level of cosmic creation, everything is in a reciprocal, dynamic relationship. Whether living or nonliving, everything within the universe is inseparable and connected in a unitary, organic relationship. Though each individual creation has its own differentiated uniqueness, it also remains part of the total universe in a reciprocal fashion. This connectedness further supports oneness among everything.

In applying this aspect of unique oneness theory to the brain, the brain must reciprocate with the external world by nature of universal reciprocity. To do this, the brain must recreate the external world internally to gain this relationship. This is accomplished by replicating the external world in its complete entirety including all the world's dimensions. Lengths, breadths, depths, weights, space, and even the time of the external world are replicated within the brain's internal environment. This is the only means by which a truly organic dynamic reciprocal relationship can be established between the brain and the external world.

The brain can recreate objects internally that are an exact replica of external objects. Indeed, this may be the most important function and fundamental aspect of the brain's role in allowing us to perceive and thrive within our environment. And while this intuitively makes perfect, logical sense, this fundamental quality of the brain's operations has never been described in prior philosophies or writing. This is what makes unique oneness theory revolutionary.

Others tend to focus on the brain's ability to rationalize and reason as its primary function, but these functions are actually secondary to the brain's ability to recreate the universe in which it operates. This ability to recreate and replicate its external environment makes it nature's most powerful force among all creation. The brain harbors this awesome potential and capacity to recreate the entire universe, and without this ability, logic and reason wouldn't be possible.

Science and medicine have described three functional states of the brain. These include wakefulness, sleep states, and dream states. The functional state where the brain can recreate and replicate its external environment, I believe, is a fourth state, which has been underappreciated and holds the key to many future revelations and discoveries about the health and function of the mind. The human brain is connected to everything else in the universe, and it reciprocates through its ability to perceive these relationships and react to them. Science continues to search for objective evidence that may demonstrate these relationships, but the lack of objective findings doesn't negate universal reciprocity.

Evidence of a New System

Science seeks to find reproducible evidence of objectivity in its everyday search for new discovery. But this hasn't been limited to simply measures of matter. In fact, scientific study has demonstrated that what appears to be nothing at all can dramatically influence matter. Without any known means of interaction, matter has been shown to be changed or altered. The studies supporting these findings range from medicine to physics.

The Medical Bureau of Lourdes, France, has been collecting data about miraculous cures since the mid-nineteenth century. A formal medical bureau of doctors routinely reviews and analyzes cases traditional means cannot explain. Each year a few cases meet their stringent criteria and are cataloged along with many others that are considered "miraculous" science, which is beyond what the laws of medicine can explain. By nature of their Catholic foundations, spiritual influence is assumed to be the casual factor.

Both doctors of religious faith and many without any faith whatsoever strictly analyze the cases in Lourdes. Every year, an average of three to five cases cannot be explained, and the catalog of such medical stories has grown to be quite tremendous. Stories of sudden resolution of paralysis after years of debilitation, sudden recoveries of end-stage dementias, and many others defy the logic of science and medicine. Without any particular way to explain how this occurs, the catalog simply keeps growing as a means to document their occurrence.

A recent review study published in the *Annals of Internal Medicine* examines more than twenty-three studies since 1999 involving more than twenty-five hundred patients for the effects of what was labeled "distant healing". As defined, distant healing in this review consisted of prayer, noncontact therapeutic touch, and mental healing methods. To be included in the review, studies had to have placebo or adequate control groups, be in a peer-reviewed publication, and consist of a clinical analysis. The purpose was to assess whether positive effects on health outcomes could be defined.

Remarkably, a majority of the reviewed studies showed positive effects. Thirteen of the studies, or 57 percent, yielded statistically significant treatment effects. Nine of the studies showed no effect. One study showed a negative effect. The authors concluded that absolute conclusions couldn't be drawn due to different methodologies, but the significant number of studies demonstrating positive outcomes warranted further examination. These findings objectively support the ability for an entity that is seemingly nonmaterial to interact with matter.

Beverly Rubik, PhD, is a researcher at the Institute of Frontier Sciences at Temple University. In 1996, she published results of different studies on bacteria that mental effects of an observer had positively influenced. In the cases, Rubik used a Salmonella species and placed these bacteria in two dishes with antibiotics. The antibiotics would inhibit the growth of the Salmonella. An observer mentally "acted upon" one dish while the other was left as a control. Interestingly the mentally affected bacteria showed an increased ability to grow compared to the control dish.

In a second set of experiments, Rubik applies a chemical known as phenol to two sets of bacteria. Again, an observer mentally acted on one set while the other was left as a control. Phenol in the amounts given was enough to immobilize but not kill the bacteria. Under microscopic analysis, the bacteria-receiving mental treatment showed continued movements in 7 percent of the bacteria after twelve minutes, while none of the control bacteria showed movement after two minutes. Both of Rubik's experiments lend objective findings that support nonmaterial interactions with matter.

Robert Jahn of Princeton University has been the subject of much debate regarding psychokinetic experiments conducted in the mid-1980s. Under the name Princeton Engineering Anomalies Research (PEAR) lab, Jahn and colleagues examined the effects of how mental activity of participants might influence the outcomes of random-number generators. Typically, random-number generators should provide an even distribution of outcomes among their number of possibilities. This would be similar to expecting an equal number of heads and tails when flipping a coin with a large number of tails.

In Jahn's experiments, data was recorded over several studies, and the effects of mental activity on altering the results of random-number generators were noted to be statistically significant. This suggested psychokinetic activity may be possible, but skeptics have continued to minimize his findings and explain the results as based on bias, statistical flaws, and small sample sizes. In 2007, the PEAR lab closed, though they concluded that their experiments had shown human intention did have a slight effect on random generating machines.

As evident from an array of scientific examinations, mental and nonmaterial interactions with material entities are supported to a great extent. The problem in gaining acceptance is that the results are often subtle and subject to harsh criticism because they challenge the norms. Accepting that something nonmaterial may influence something material would upset the established foundations on which science is based. But is such a new paradigm to be so rejected if it indeed may eventually lead us to a greater knowledge of reality and consciousness? Isn't the search for truth the underlying goal of both scientific and religious efforts?

Unique Oneness Theory and Entanglement

To digress into physics again, the process of entanglement has been elucidated, which provides some additional insight into how other interactions in the universe may influence our bodies. This further supports how every particle, molecule, and atom is integrally related to every other. Though far from being understood, entanglement suggests two items don't have to be near each other to have an influence; in fact, they don't even have to interact temporally.

Initially, entanglement was demonstrated in photons of lights. One photon at a higher frequency could be split into two photons of lower frequency. Because of their relationship, the frequencies of the two photons were interdependent on each other because energy is always conserved and maintained constant within the universe. However, a similar phenomenon has been shown with electrons within an atom. The spins of two electrons are entangled together and dependent on each other.

As an example, take a hydrogen molecule. In the two hydrogen atoms, each has one electron. As the molecule is formed, one electron spins in one direction, and the other electron spins in the exact opposite direction. These two electrons are said to be entangled. What recent physics experiments have shown is that even if these electrons are separated from each other, they continue to maintain their direction of spin. No matter the distance, they remain entangled.

Taking this a step further, Dr. Robin Kelly in his book *The Human Antenna* describes each of our cells as containing similar abilities. The cells of our bodies serve as semiconductors that transmit information to other cells and receive information from various signals around us. But using the concept of entanglement, the cells don't need to have direct interaction to be influenced. Instead, they are entangled with everything else in the universe and react to changes accordingly. In this fashion, Kelly describes how stress, acupuncture, and a variety of holistic therapeutic techniques affect our bodies because our cells and DNA are entangled with other happenings occurring everywhere.

Our bodies are composed of fifty trillion cells, and each cell is made up of molecules. Molecules are then made up of atoms. Of these billions of atoms existing in our bodies, two-thirds of these are hydrogen atoms. In fact, 90 percent of all atoms in the universe are hydrogen atoms. Magnetic resonance imaging (MRI) has used this knowledge to create images of our bodies with incredible detail. If each of these hydrogen atoms is entangled and its electrons are interconnected, then one can realize the interconnectivity and oneness of everything.

Although atoms are incredibly small, they are in reality filled with a vast amount of space. The amount of space protons, neutrons, and electrons occupy makes a very small percentage of an atom, which leaves a significant amount of space unoccupied. Or is it?

Suppose 90 percent of each hydrogen atom was 'empty space' and 90 percent of the world including our bodies was composed of hydrogen atoms. Then that would conclude that more than 80 percent of all of existence was empty space at a minimum. Now suppose this space wasn't truly empty at all. Instead, this space was the very essence of the nonmaterial. Perhaps this space is where consciousness actually resides.

For centuries, we have been formally and scientifically examining the workings of a body. The more and more we learn, the more intricate detail we come to see about our bodies. In reducing our field of vision to smaller and smaller areas of study, something paradoxical is happening. We are discovering that our inner space that composes our cells and bodies is remarkably more like "outer space" with each additional piece of information gained. With such great vastness of space, why do we insist on focusing on the small amount of matter within it?

The phenomenon of entanglement highlights how tiny electrons and pieces of matter can be integrally related regardless of their closeness to each other in distance and time. This is unusual and defies what is traditionally understood about interactions of particles. But somehow these electrons "talk" to each other and react to each other. In much the same way, so do our bodies. Like the concept of entanglement, unique oneness theory holds that all the universe is one and is integrated together into reality. Entanglement is simply another observation that supports this view.

Perceptual Capacity

As a matter of common questions, the topic of whether humans are the only species to carry the capacity to perceive and replicate their external environment must be addressed. According to unique oneness theory, this capacity is selective not only to human beings but also to all forms of living species. From the lowest species to the highest, the capacity to perceive the external world through recreating a replica of the universe exists.

Differences in degree exist, but the basic capacity among living species remains. Lower species don't have as sophisticated a central nervous system that would allow the same level of replication or perception as humans, but they can recreate a simpler version of the external world according to the brain they have. As species evolve through the evolutionary process, the extent of their perceptual capacity increases, reaching its greatest extent within human beings. But evolution is still progressing, and as humans, we still don't know our supreme potential and capacity in the future.

An important principle of perceptual capacity is that it distinguishes the living from the nonliving. The ability and capacity to recreate the external environment of the universe define what is living and what is nonliving between matter and consciousness and between living intelligence and artificial intelligence. Matter that isn't conscious and living doesn't have the ability to recreate the external world. Likewise, the most intricate artificial intelligence machine cannot replicate the world around it internally. As we move into future chapters, these concepts will be expanded on to characterize perceptual capacity more fully.

The descriptions have established the platform on which unique oneness theory holds its key tenets. And on this platform, an innovative approach to health care can be considered. While a great deal of physics and philosophy has been discussed, this has simply been a means to support how unique oneness theory perceives reality and views how changes in our current beliefs can yield new revelations. However, the current goal of unique oneness theory from a practical standpoint is to apply this new way of thinking to clinical health.

To consider therapeutic attempts, explaining current healthy and pathological states under the rubric of unique oneness theory is important. This perspective will diverge a bit from traditional medicine but certainly embraces clinical traditions and known observations as part of its viewpoint. In this way, this new approach is inclusive and not exclusive. By enlarging the scope with which to view health, new openings to treatment and diagnosis can be established, leading to greater health for all.

CHAPTER 8

Abnormal Perceptions

When we accept that a unique perceptual ability exists for each of us despite a universal monistic reality, it becomes apparent that aberrancy may occur. Clearly what may be "real" to one person may not be accepted as fact by another. But exactly how is any reality defined as being normal or abnormal? If unique perceptions are inherently present, what criteria can be used to determine whether one perception is abnormal or simply within the variation of normal uniqueness?

From a sociological viewpoint, normalcy is defined by what the majority perceive. Similar to a statistical analysis, deviations from the norms are identified based on whether a perception falls outside an acceptable range. For scientific study, these ranges are mathematically defined. But for human perception, the boundaries aren't as clear. This accounts for a spectrum of conditions that form the transition between normal human psychology and pathological psychology.

Examples of this exist in many instances. For example, the transition from appropriate concern to mild anxiety, obsessive compulsive disorder, schizoid personality, and paranoid schizophrenia may all represent small changes in the degree of perceptual aberrations. resulting in different clinical presentations. Approaching the assessment of these conditions from a viewpoint of unique oneness theory allows a fresh perspective and provides opportunities for a few insights.

Several possibilities exist that may account for these aberrations and cause a unique perception of reality to be altered outside the realm of normalcy. Some of these possibilities will be considered in this chapter and thus lay the foundation for discussing more specific clinical conditions and treatments in the chapters to follow.

Consciousness Revisited

In earlier chapters of this book, consciousness was defined from a philosophical standpoint. In this light, consciousness has come to mean something different than the way many scientists use the term. For example, physicians refer to consciousness as more a level of alertness and awareness of the external experience. Therefore, if a person suffers some type of brain injury and goes into a coma, his or her level of consciousness is stated to be severely impaired.

In this setting, the term *consciousness* defines what is known as an objective consciousness. Objective consciousness is concerned with an awareness and perception of the world around us. It is concerned with the external appearance of our bodies as objects. The entire replication of our external world depends on a conscious awareness of all the incoming sensory stimuli we experience moment by moment and on the ability to integrate this information. Without a doubt, the normal function of our neurons and neural networks is crucial to this objective form of consciousness.

In contrast, or perhaps in collaboration, there is a second component of consciousness. This is referred to as subjective consciousness. Subjective consciousness is concerned with the subjective experience of perceptions and the external world as it affects the self. For example, objective consciousness is required to create the replica of reality for us to perceive reality. However, subjective consciousness allows us to award value to this perception. Value is more than simply a set of emotions or thoughts. Instead, subjective consciousness includes facets of morality, justice, and other intangible constructs that each individual awards the reality being perceived. Subjective consciousness, rather than residing within neural networks, thus exists outside this process.

Certainly, the ability to have subjective consciousness depends in part on objective consciousness. However, it's impossible to state that some level of subjective consciousness doesn't exist as objective consciousness declines. The debate over the value of life in a vegetative patient in part raises this issue. Not only are there arguments that the individual might not have some miraculous cure, but there also exists the possibility that subjective consciousness remains, even though objective consciousness is critically impaired. The answers to these questions are unavailable for the simple reason that measuring subjective consciousness is beyond the scope of today's science.

Gerald Edelman talks a great deal about conscious experience in his written works. Conscious experience as described is being widely distributed among many neurons that interact rapidly to create consciousness and perception. The more a sequence is practiced, the more automatic it becomes and the less conscious the action or perception may be. In this setting, Edelman is referring to objective consciousness. Subjective consciousness, which then assigns value to these sequences from a higher ethical sense of meaning, has yet to be localized to cerebral or neurologic tissues.

In the subsequent descriptions regarding perceptual abnormalities, it is implied that the perceptual abnormalities that occur are predominantly due to disturbances in sensory information or objective consciousness. This involves receiving information through neural structures about our world as well as the neural integration and analysis of this information in creating the unique perception of reality. It doesn't imply a disturbance in subjective consciousness. However, as will be eventually discussed, the use of subjective consciousness in investigating and treating perceptual disturbances offers new opportunities for the future. The interface where objective consciousness and subjective consciousness meet is an area worth serious study.

Simple Perceptual Impairments

Some may prefer to use the term *primary impairments* rather than *simple impairments*; however, the complexity of secondary perceptual abilities justifies the distinction of impairments according to their intricacies. Regardless of which term is preferred, the impairments discussed here are typically more apparent and explainable. The resultant dysfunction in perceptual ability is therefore more easily accepted and understood.

The easiest dysfunction in perception to appreciate is when primary sensory modalities aren't properly functioning. The ability of one who is blind or visually impaired (especially if from birth) isn't the same as one who has normal visual abilities. The same applies for those who are hearing impaired or have altered sensory input from other modalities. The inability of a person to process normal information through peripheral nerve pathways naturally limits the degree with which the perceptual system of the brain can replicate reality.

Despite these primary limitations, people with simple impairments of sensory inputs understand their limitations as does society. Aberrancy in perception that falls in line with the impairment is justified and rationalized. A scientific explanation exists because the anatomy, physiology, and pathology are known. In other words, the primary handicap results in a perceptual handicap.

When we move up the hierarchy of perceptual anatomy, the integration of sensory inputs must take place next in order or replicate reality for the individual. This, of course, occurs within the central nervous system and brain. These impairments of cerebral function limit perceptual abilities. A person who suffers brain trauma or is born with cerebral palsy may have significant impairments in the ability to integrate information. Again, it's perfectly understandable why unique perceptual limitations occur in those individuals.

Though primary integration of sensory inputs about our environment is essential to perceptual abilities, the capacity to compare new sensory information to old sensory information is also a key part of this process. A child, of course, has less experience than an adult. Therefore, there is a lesser ability to interpret and comparatively make sense of sensory information for the child. Intuitively, we know this and accept that a child's perception of a situation isn't as "real" as our own.

People with memory impairments have a similar problem. They may have experiential data stored within their memory, but the access of that information to allow normal perceptual processing is impaired. Mild senile forgetfulness of the elderly is common enough that this perceptual confusion that occurs on occasion is overlooked. It is accepted as a normal feature of senility and thus isn't necessarily categorized as a perceptual dysfunction. Only when it gets to the point of impaired functional living do we begin to name it a pathology or dementia. Once this occurs, the complexity of the impairment is less easy to understand.

The final category of what would be considered a simple perceptual impairment would be changes in perceptual capacity. To an extent, injuries or age-related differences in physical and mental function can alter this perceptual capacity as has been described. However, in the truest sense, natural differences exist in perceptual capacities based on other factors. An animal such as a dog or cat has the capacity to perceive the environment and its body just as we do. But as discussed in the last chapter, the degree with which this perception occurs is less advanced than that of human beings. Therefore, we don't expect an animal to be able to perceive its environment with the same degree of complexity that we do.

To some degree, this same perceptual capacity is influenced by intellectual achievement and by experience. Consider a magician, for example. A trick is performed that demonstrates a person disappearing into thin air. Perceptually, the person appears to vanish right before our eyes. However, once the magician reveals the trick, we can appreciate the illusion of the perception and focus on what really happened. In other words, our perceptual capacity changed as our understanding, intellect, and experience did. We are now able to more accurately perceive reality.

History has numerous accounts where misperception of reality occurred because of limited knowledge and/or experience. Allegations of witchcraft and sorcery, claims that the world was flat, and the egocentric view of the galaxy are some of the more obvious examples of this. As each generation gains new insights into reality, universal perception changes. What we perceive as real today may be quite different in the next decade and century. Therefore, there should always be a degree of caution as to what is considered normal perception and abnormal perception at any given time.

Because the impairments discussed in this section are straightforward and easily understood, these have been identified as simple impairments in the perceptual process. A person who has a disability has obvious limitations in perceiving the environment accurately, as does a child, an animal, or someone with limited information or intellect. Rarely do these situations create confusion about why the perceptual process is different from the norm. Regardless, unique oneness theory provides a new way of examining these impairments and potentially in treating their limited abilities.

These aspects will be addressed later under the therapeutic sections of this book. For now, it is sufficient to understand that these perceptual impairments are all around us every day. Because we understand the science behind the impairment, we accept these without resistance. This may not necessarily be the case with more complex impairments.

Complex Perceptual Impairments

Unlike simple impairments, complex perceptual impairments are more intricate and involved from a psychological and emotional perspective. This doesn't mean a scientific or physiological process isn't present, accounting for the impairment. However, the mechanisms by which these impairments occur are only partially known at best, leaving a great deal of room for speculation, judgment, and opinion. While some have been defined to a great extent as diseases or medical disorders, others have not. This opens the door for different thoughts about whether a perception is more or less accurate overall.

For example, manic depression is a defined medical illness in the field of psychiatry. It has multiple symptoms that may be present, including perceptual abnormalities; and if enough of these symptoms are present, then the formal diagnosis is made. In addition, large numbers of patients labeled with this disorder have responded favorably to medications and have shown characteristic changes on some functional imaging studies, such as PET scans and functional MRIs. All this leads us to understand that manic depression is a medical illness.

On the other hand, a schizoid personality has no clear objective examination findings to support its causation and categorization as a scientific disease. These patients carry typical personality traits and behaviors, and they indeed have odd perceptions of their environment. But objective examinations of neurological function, physical function, and other testing remains normal in the majority.

Both manic-depressive patients and schizoid-personality patients have perceptual difficulties, but one is considered more of a neuropsychological disorder while the other is perceived as more of a psychological development disorder. The complexity of these conditions is what creates the ambiguity and lack of complete understanding of the conditions. By looking at these conditions as a perceptual impairment under the rubric of unique oneness theory, new insights into both conditions can be gained and new therapies tested.

As mentioned in the previous chapter, a fourth state of perceptual replication can offer the chance to look at many psychiatric and neurological conditions from a new lens. Medicine seeks to explain all conditions from only one state of consciousness, which is the awake state. Dream states and sleep states are unable to be examined objectively, since the person dreaming or sleeping cannot provide information. However, it's possible to train someone to appreciate his or her state of perceptual replication as it is happening. This subject will be considered later in the book.

The following are some considerations that may account for more complex perceptual abnormalities that fall outside the realm of normalcy. Certainly, there are others, but these categories will serve to demonstrate what unique oneness theory proposes as potential discretions of study moving forward.

Inability to Accept Perceptual Data

While simple impairments have been described in accepting or receiving sensory information about the environment, more complex impairments also exist. These may result from psychological limitations, emotional limitations, or limitations we have yet to identify. Whatever the underlying reason, sensory information presented to our perceptual systems is unable to be properly integrated into an accurate perception of reality. As a result, aberrancies in perception are created instead.

Suppose an individual suffers emotional abuse as a child. The abuse is severe enough that anything appearing similar in nature evokes a deep emotional and mental reaction. Regardless of whether this reaction is part of the person's awareness, the reaction may inhibit a situation from being accurately perceived. The emotional or mental feeling evoked by acknowledging this perception may be too overwhelming and in turn prevent accurate perception. Despite accurate sensory input and the ability to integrate this input with experience, knowledge, and memories, other aspects keep the actual perception from being accepted.

An important question arises as to where this inability to accept this reality develops. Is it part of our cognitive pathways and emotional cortex? Or instead is it at a consciousness level? According to unique oneness theory, the emotional memory content resides within cerebral structures, but the conscious or even subconscious suppression of this information and the inability to accurately perceive the current situation reside outside these same tissues. Consciousness itself plays a large role in this setting, and by using consciousness to become aware of these perceptual roadblocks, improvement can be made.

Emotional trauma is simply one example of many things that may interfere with the ability to accurately accept reality despite normal sensory inputs and integrated functions of the nervous system.

Other instances may involve a refusal to accept reality because it's against what one strongly believes to be true. Or it may result from a limited ability to perceive a situation because the information is too overwhelming. Major changes in existing databases within the mind would be required to make this perceptual leap.

Unlike the last section, which described simplistic limitations, these impairments are much more complex. Multiple components may be involved that interfere with accurate perception, and sorting these out into some type of rational explanation can be difficult. However, as these components are elucidated, accurate perception can then proceed as the individual understands why the roadblocks exist. Awareness and consciousness dissolve the impairments and limitations, and perception can normalize.

Conflicting Information

Despite sensory inputs being able to function normally and our brains being able to process and integrate this information, on occasion information and data arrive that are antagonistic. One set of data conflicts with another set of data according to our perceptual capacity. Therefore, a decision must be made to rationalize the conflict and accept one of the data sets or a partial combination of both. How this distinction is made affects the perception we have of reality.

The magician described earlier is one example of conflicting inputs. We have come to know it's impossible for a person to disappear into thin air, yet all our sensory inputs indicate that this indeed has happened. Does the rational logic that comes from years of experience and knowledge prevail, or do we throw that aside and accept what we are apparently seeing? For most of us, logic prevails.

In the movie *The Soloist*, a young man who is a musical genius begins to suffer auditory hallucinations while enrolled at Juilliard

School of Music. He is initially aware of the irrational aspect of the voices he hears but is unable to shut them out. Progressively the voices begin to affect his ability to play music. He receives not only external auditory inputs but also internal auditory inputs. These conflicting inputs create perceptual problems for the man despite his initial ability to distinguish real from unreal. Perception is distorted as a result, and as the disorder worsens, the illness of paranoid schizophrenia reveals itself.

Abnormal perceptual pathologies occur when conflicting sensory data is received in some instances. Every day in normal perceptual functioning, some information conflicts with other data, whether concurrently received or between current information and what is already stored in our brains. These conflicts are resolved based on logical conclusions, but these conclusions aren't always completely accurate when compared to reality. This provides the uniqueness we each perceive. Simply gather eyewitness reports of a car accident from several different people, and you will understand that differences in perceptions occur easily despite a constant reality.

When we apply this concept to pathological states of perception, we can see a new perspective in understanding how specific symptoms occur. Visual and auditory hallucinations are obvious in the way they conflict with normal sensory inputs about our environment. However, contradictory emotional reactions to life situations can cause the same perceptual conflict. For example, a person may interact with someone who is asking routine questions, but an internal emotional reaction awards a paranoid flavor to the questions in perceptual processing and causes anxiousness. The individual must resolve the conflict between what is factually apparent and what he or she is feeling. Depending on which side of the conflict is more powerful, the resulting perception may or may not be close to reality.

Mental health, in particular, can be analyzed from a viewpoint of conflicting informational content. This, of course, doesn't preclude whatever underlying anatomical or physiological abnormality may be present. But it does offer a new way of assessing where the symptoms and perceptual dysfunctions occur and how to possibly intervene in alleviating them. This may allow patients and therapists new approaches in ameliorating perceptual conflicts.

Lack of Informational Feedback

Whether you realize it, your perception of the environment is constantly receiving feedback. As you take your hand and reach out to grab a piece of paper, every gradation of movement sends feedback information to the brain. This allows the movement to be finetuned so the exact movement is completed. Without this feedback information, perception of the environment may be distorted.

Our nervous system requires a constant stream of informational input to maintain a constant and relatively accurate perception of our environment. The replication of an internal image of reality is created from sensory inputs, but it is maintained by continued inputs and feedback from our own interaction with the environment. In this way, errors in perception can be minimized, and the replication of reality in our perception can be as accurate as possible.

This can be demonstrated in people who have been deprived of sensory inputs completely for days at a time. In concentration camps of prisoners, complete isolation from light, noise, and mobility eventually starts to cause hallucinatory effects. Auditory noises are heard that are without an external stimulus. Images and shadows appears that aren't triggered by real movements. Internally, within our perceptual system, an attempt to replicate the external world occurs, even though sensory information is limited. The lack of input and feedback begins to trigger aberrant perceptions to occur.

To some extent, some scientists and physicians theorize that dreams during REM sleep reflect similar perceptual creations in the absence of sensory input and feedback. During this activated brain state of sleep, images and scenarios similar to reality are created. However, we realize these images and dreams are all internally constructed. As we awake, we accept and understand it was simply a dream. The wakeful feedback we receive from our environment allows us to understand and accept this.

It may well be possible that the lack of feedback in some individuals causes perceptual dysfunctions, even when they are awake. Also, some individuals may require greater feedback to allow accurate perceptions of their environments. When this fails to occur, distortions of reality surface. In some children with autism and/or cerebral palsy, one form of therapy increases tactile stimulation through rubbing or massaging their arms or body. This tactile feedback appears to have a soothing effect on their behavior. The same has been found true for children with attention deficit disorder.

Though the interaction of feedback about our environment and our ability to accurately perceive it isn't well known, these factors indicate that this area is worth further investigation. As described in unique oneness theory, the ability to provide greater input and feedback could allow our perceptual system to replicate our external environment to a better degree. Likewise, using our consciousness to encourage this process may be quite therapeutic in some perceptual disorders.

Lack of Inhibitory Processes

In the normal perceptual process of the human mind, a replica of the environment is created through a series of excitatory and inhibitory signals. For example, an excitatory signal created by the touch of an area of one's skin is accompanied by inhibitory signals from adjacent skin regions. This serves to enhance the precise region of sensory input and helps us localize where we are being touched. An intermingling between inhibitory and excitatory signals is constantly ongoing within our nervous system, helping us analyze reality and create our own replica of our world.

Without this balance between excitation and inhibition, our ability to accurately perceive our environment becomes impaired. An imbalance can occur due to hyperstimulation from the environment, causing sensory overload, or the imbalance may be the result of an internal disorder. Either way, the lack of inhibition can cause an excess of excitatory messages that impairs the ability to create an accurate portrayal of reality. Neuroscience has demonstrated many disorders where this imbalance exists. Epilepsy, Parkinson's disease, and some pain syndromes are common examples.

In unique oneness theory, the opportunity exists to view this phenomenon from another perspective, particularly for mental conditions. While seizures may result in neuron hyperexcitability and a lack of inhibition, perceptual conditions can also occur in a similar fashion. For example, in a patient with bipolar disorder, who is suffering from an episode of mania, the lack of inhibitory control creates an excess of excitatory stimuli. Perception then becomes altered as a result. Mental interpretations of reality become disconnected as thoughts jump from one topic to another without any evidence of rational connection. Speech becomes excessive and explosive. And even visual and auditory hallucinations may develop if the excitation is severe enough.

Through techniques that make one aware of these lack of inhibitory controls, conscious control can assist in redirecting perception toward a more accurate replica of the real world. This certainly may not climate the need for medication assistance, but cognitive therapies may offer adjunctive treatments for perceptual disorders in this setting. This alone is empowering to an individual who is suffering perceptual difficulties.

A similar perspective could be considered during the depressed phase of the same bipolar patient. A relative lack of excitatory stimuli and/or an excessive number of inhibitory signals could lead to altered perceptions of the environment that lead to the symptoms of depression. Hyper somnolence, lack of appetite, lack of energy, and a sad mood support an imbalance between inhibitory and excitatory stimuli. Again, acknowledging this from a perceptual standpoint and trying to actively correct this imbalance through cognitive therapy could lead to nonpharmacological treatments that help correct reality perception.

Unique oneness theory doesn't conflict with scientific and medical discoveries that account for various neurological and psychiatric conditions but is actually congruent with current knowledge. The theory simply states that in creating an internal replica of our outside world, cognitive awareness and active consciousness play a part in self-correcting perceptual dysfunctions. Because consciousness exists outside neural tissues, using consciousness to assist in therapeutic endeavors makes logical sense.

The Spectrum between "Normal" and "Abnormal" Perceptual Impairments

Defining normal perception versus abnormal or pathological perception is difficult in some situations. We all have our unique perception of reality. One person may perceive a situation as threatening while another doesn't. One may perceive details of an event completely different from another. But these are simply the uniqueness of the perception given the minor variations in sensory inputs, neural processing, and neural integration we each have. All are based on one reality, and all are within a range of what we as a society determine to be normal.

As time moves forward, society has the potential to change how reality is perceived. Advances in science, technology, and philosophy change the way we human beings see our environment, and therefore perception of the same reality can change from one generation to the next. Normal perception is therefore defined by social consensus rather than by precise observational recordings alone. In other words, our perceptual capacity is only as advanced as our knowledge of the ultimate reality.

With this in mind, it is completely understandable that nonmaterial entities exist in reality, but we aren't equipped or advanced enough to perceive these entities at this time. Viruses and bacteria existed long before the invention of the microscope, but we were unable to perceive them because we weren't equipped to do so. The fact that science and medicine measure entities based only on energy and matter doesn't preclude that another entity may exist. One day we may indeed to able to perceive this entity or entities, whether directly or indirectly. This unperceived locale indeed may be where true consciousness and awareness reside.

Regardless of the variations of "normal" perceptions that occur in our society, aberrant perceptions of reality clearly occur and reflect pathological conditions. The spectrum between normal and abnormal isn't a definitive boundary. Instead a gray area exists, bridging these two ends of the spectrum. Just as blood pressure measurements travel from normal readings to borderline hypertension to essential hypertension, perceptions follow a similar procession. At a baseline level, a mild degree of unique variation of perception exists. But as the degree of aberrancy increases, these variations are eventually labeled as perceptual disorders or even neuropsychiatric disorders.

When we keep in mind that a clear line of demarcation doesn't exist and that we all have variations of perception of reality, it's easy to accept that increasing awareness of our own perceptual processes can help us gain a better understanding of ourselves. In this manner, perceptual assessment and therapies can be invoked in many medical and even nonmedical conditions to help improve quality of living. This is what unique oneness theory offers.

In the subsequent chapter, we will examine some specific medical conditions where perceptual disturbances play a significant role in the symptomatology. Detailing these specific disorders will help apply the general areas of perceptual abnormalities discussed in this chapter. And it will also help open the door for other areas of application and analysis. Not only does unique oneness theory have the potential of helping us gain a better understanding of these disorders, but it will also provide new chances to give adjunctive therapy for these conditions.

CHAPTER 9

Applying Unique Oneness Theory to Specific Disorders

N ow that we have discussed general concepts under the umbrella of unique oneness theory, which result in abnormal perceptions, specific instances can provide a better grasp and understanding of key processes involved. And by understanding greater specifics, we can begin to incorporate therapies and research that specifically tailor to an individual's disorder and set of symptoms.

Until now, the traditional view of many disorders regarding perception is that the nervous system is altered in a physical or chemical way to alter sensory processing and integration of these stimuli. Therefore, medicine has tended to focus on medication and surgery to a greater extent than other therapeutic endeavors. Psychotherapy and education are tools used, but in many instances, these are given a back seat. Likewise, expansion of these tools of treatment and area of study receives less attention than quick-fix interventions, such as drugs and operations.

Unique oneness theory offers a chance to expand both educational and cognitive therapies by employing a new perspective in the development of reality perception. The concepts of uniqueness and unification of reality can be used to facilitate self-empowerment and self-control over one's disease. Additionally, unique oneness theory provides a chance to explore how subject consciousness may influence objective consciousness in conditions where perception is flawed. In this way, the theory seeks to broaden the scope of information and interventions rather than replace current concepts.

To appreciate this in greater detail, a few select medical illnesses that involve perceptual disturbances will be discussed. Theoretical explanation for symptomatology will be provided as postulated under the concepts of unique oneness theory, and concurrently some suggestion of how these concepts may be applied in therapy will be made. These points are theoretical and deserve rigorous study despite the limitations present in measuring such aspects of intervention. Regardless, this will serve as a starting point with which to pursue this new perspective.

Bipolar Disorder

Bipolar disorder, also known as manic depression, affects more than ten million people in the United States alone. Additionally, the disorder affects men and women in adolescence and young adulthood, commonly causing them to struggle with this lifelong disease. Though ascribed as a mood disorder, bipolar disorder involves multiple perceptual difficulties, as manifested in an array of common symptoms. These symptoms include a variety of perceptual problems, including altered thought patterns, impaired risk, assessment, and even overt hallucinations.

For the most part, the discussion here will be limited to these perceptual symptoms. The presence of mood disturbances, which range from depression to mania, are certainly the hallmark of the disorder, but perceptions affect mood and vice versa. The interplay between perceptions and mood is noteworthy. Mood is created through perceptual stimulation of neural networks that evoke emotional responses or connect with emotional memories. In some instances, mood is generated internally in the absence of these stimuli, but perceptions still have the potential even here to influence mood.

Altered Thought Patterns

The most common feature of bipolar disorder is labeled "flight of ideas." This symptom complex is composed of racing thoughts that occur so quickly that the ability to perceptually integrate them into a coherent context is difficult. A person in the manic phase of the disorder thus appears to be leaping from one thought to the next without any rational connection. Interestingly, individuals with flight of ideas often inherently believe their conversation and thoughts are cohesive and rational. Their perception of reality is significantly altered, yet internally they still believe it is accurate.

By applying unique oneness theory, it's apparent that the unique perception of reality has been altered outside what is considered normal by society's terms. Logical premises and conclusions are absent in the individual's speech and thought. However, reality is the same. The presumed dysfunction occurs within the objective consciousness of the individual who, despite intact sensory stimuli, is no longer able to integrate the information properly. The volume or speed of excitatory stimuli drowns the individual's ability to accurately perceive his or her world.

From a different and quite opposite perspective, the situation is nearly reserved when a bipolar patient is in a depressed phase of the illness. With overt depression, the most common thought disturbance is a loss of attention and concentration. Sometimes this can be so severe that symptoms mimic a dementing illness. In this situation, sensory stimuli are again presumed to be functioning normally, but the ability to integrate the signals into an accurate replica and perception of reality is hindered. The inhibition of excitatory stimuli and information processing prevents full accuracy as objective consciousness is suppressed. The perception is still based on the same true reality, but it is pathologically unique to the individual because of the existing bipolar condition.

Impaired Risk Assessment

Another common symptom during the manic phase of bipolar disorder includes a greater degree of impulsiveness and increased risk taking. While this may not seem directly related to perception, perception is an integral part of the ability to judge and predict situational outcomes. For example, suppose an individual is at work and having a disagreement over a problem's solution with a supervisor. Instead of the conversation being constructive and calm, the individual with bipolar disease begins to yell and threaten the supervisor because he doesn't share the same view. The result is that the individual is suspended from work. The assessment of the situation was flawed from the beginning and resulted in negative behavior and a bad outcome.

What happened in this situation perceptually? Perhaps perception was flawed at several levels. The conversation may have been inaccurately perceived as a confrontation instead of a constructive dialogue. The projected outcome of an argument may have been underestimated. The perception of a personal attack instead of a topical disagreement may have been perceived as reality. In each of these cases, perception is abnormal, and the result can cause the symptoms described.

While chemical and physical changes within the nervous system may have affected objective consciousness and perception, understanding that a perceptual disturbance exists can facilitate this individual to have greater control. Simply knowing that the perception of the conversation may have been inaccurate could allow a person to alter his or her behavior despite the replica of reality being perceived. The perception of reality is unique to this individual, and because of altered integration abilities of sensory data, this perception doesn't meet the social range of normalcy in perceiving the one true reality. Unique oneness theory not only helps explain why this is happening but can offer self-therapy tools to help guide reality perception back toward the social norms.

Overt Hallucinations in Bipolar Disorder

Though less common than other psychiatric conditions, hallucinations occur in some patients with bipolar disorder. Auditory hallucinations are most common, but visual and tactile (sensory) hallucinations also occur. Because the primary disturbance in bipolar disorder is located in the brain and central nervous system, the perceptual parts of the peripheral nervous system are intact. The false interpretation of sensory stimuli and the interjection of false images, sounds, or feelings into the patient's perception is what accounts for these hallucinatory phenomena.

Hallucinations can occur during both manic and depressed phases of this disorder, though manic-related hallucinations are more common. Presumably, aberrant physical and chemical changes cause dysfunction in the perceptual networks of the brain. Many patients have a degree of awareness that these hallucinatory events aren't consistent with reality despite their very real appearance. These are the patients who can benefit the most from understanding the premises of unique oneness theory.

Cognitive and behavioral training helps the individual establish some degree of control, and that is the underlying purpose of unique oneness theory techniques. Environmental feedback to test hallucinatory phenomena can provide an objective sense of reality, which can be compared against perceived reality. While this may not significantly alter the presence of hallucinations, it can provide incentive to take medication, seek treatment help, or avoid mistaken behaviors. All these can provide adjunctive benefits for the patient suffering from bipolar disorder.

Alzheimer's Dementia

Almost everyone knows somebody affected by this unfortunate disorder. As the most common dementia known, Alzheimer's dementia manifests itself through a variety of symptoms, including perceptual disturbances. In addition to short-term memory loss, perceptual disturbances in time, space, and objective clarity are all common features Alzheimer's patients often experience. These are often evident early in the course of the disease when intervention can be most rewarding.

Unique oneness theory can provide therapeutic benefits to patients suffering from this disorder by educating them about their perceptual dysfunctions and guiding them toward more accurate reality perceptions. Despite the assimilation and integration of sensory information being awry, perceptual self-correction through feedback and self-awareness experiences can be achieved. While specific experiences will be described in the subsequent chapter, an overview of symptom-specific effects provided by unique oneness theory will be described here.

Temporal Misperceptions

Interestingly, changes in the perception of time occur normally with aging to some extent. Some researchers have found that older individuals have a faster internal clock than others (though this finding may be influenced by the level of literacy). In Alzheimer's patients, these same phenomena often appear, but the speed of the internal clock may be accelerated or delayed. As a result, the perception of how long or how quickly a task may take is skewed and can affect daily performance.

The reason Alzheimer's patients suffer such disturbances results from the pathology known to take place. The temporal lobes of the brain are commonly affected early in Alzheimer's disease, which is where the perception of time is believed to be located. As these regions deteriorate, the ability to accurately perceive time fails, and misjudgments occur. Once again, this is where unique oneness theory can provide assistance.

Especially in early Alzheimer's disease, providing a patient with feedback about the length of time something takes can be of help in reestablishing accuracy of time perception. Because of overt brain pathology, the patient may be unable to rely on natural brain pathways in this regard. However, unique oneness theory can teach a patient other means to assess time through bypassing affected brain regions. Through educating a patient about the presence of flawed time perception, acceptance of this aspect of the disorder is more likely. And because failure to recognize symptoms is a significant part of Alzheimer's, this alone can be very helpful in providing care.

Through understanding that time perception isn't consistent with true reality, patients can begin to rely on other tools (watches, clocks, and so forth) to provide guidance through their day. In time, use of these tools and other forms of feedback and cognitive exercises may allow better independent function in accurate time perception.

Spatial Misperception

Like temporal misperception, spatial misperception commonly occurs in early Alzheimer's dementia. This results from pathological involvement of the temporal lobes, particularly on the right side of the brain. Various drawing exercises have demonstrated the presence of poor spatial functioning, showing altered spatial planning, impaired distribution of symbols within a pattern, and poor recognition of three-dimensional forms. The patients' visual system is still functioning accurately, but the ability to recreate the three-dimensional replica of reality within the brain is flawed.

As the disorder progresses, getting patients to recognize the impairment in spatial perception can be difficult. Therefore, early intervention is important. If applications of unique oneness theory can be applied during early stages of Alzheimer's retraining of healthier brain regions to understand and recognize, this perceptual disturbance can aid other treatments over a longer period. Teaching patients where and why spatial misperception occurs is important, as is providing a way to receive additional feedback to help correct the disturbance. These efforts can have real implications in improving activities of daily living.

Perceptual Clarity

As Alzheimer's disease advances, symptoms begin to include more overt perceptual disturbances. Initially poor interpretations of situations lead to mild confusion about the details of an event. Eventually, overt delusions and even hallucinations can occur, accompanied by personality changes. All these represent a spectrum of changes that occur as the temporal lobes of the brain and other regions become increasingly affected. As with most perceptual disturbances, unique oneness theory has the best chance of effectiveness when introduced early in the disorder.

Hopefully through descriptions in this book, it is apparent that each of us has a unique perception of reality, regardless of where it falls in the standard deviations of the social norm. The goal in

Alzheimer's patients is to make them aware that their perception has fallen outside this standard deviation by providing feedback from the environment itself and through other people. As long as a degree of mental clarity exists, educating patients about their misperceptions is possible. This then opens the door for therapeutic interventions.

As the disorder progresses, these techniques devised under unique oneness theory may become more difficult because the ability of self-awareness and rational clarity is lost. Combining these therapies with pharmacological treatments may be still advantageous. Applying unique oneness theory concepts in this situation may allow lower dosages of medication to be used and also reduce disease complications. Future research is needed to determine whether these techniques might even delay disease progression through an internal, natural defense mechanism.

Schizophrenia

More than 1 percent of the population suffers from schizophrenia, and this disorder affects mostly young men and women in the prime of their life. The hallmarks of the disorder include a variety of symptoms often categorized as positive, negative, or cognitive symptoms. Hallucinations, delusions, and disorganized thoughts are the most prominent positive symptoms. Negative symptoms include flat affect, blunted social interaction, and an overall lack of pleasure or satisfaction in life. Lastly, cognitive symptoms include poor attention and concentration as well as poor decision-making abilities. Of these symptoms, positive symptoms primarily fall within the realm of perceptual disturbances.

Definitive causes of schizophrenia have yet to be elucidated, but clearly genetic risk is present is most patients combined with some type of environmental stressor. Functional radiology studies demonstrate changes in the temporal lobes and frontal lobes; these correlate well with the changes in personality and perception described. Like the other disorders already discussed, there appears to be some type of organic disease affecting the brain's ability to integrate sensory information into an accurate replica of reality. As a result, perceptual disturbances occur. In this section, positive symptoms will be addressed in relation to unique oneness theory and how this theory can assist in therapeutic endeavors.

Overt Hallucinations of Schizophrenia

The psychotic hallucinations of schizophrenia are often more intense than those of other psychiatric disorders. Often a strong component of paranoia is present, associated with voices being heard or with visual aberrations. There is a foreboding sensation that the auditory or visual hallucinations are instructing the patient to harm himself or herself or do common terrible actions, and that somehow he or she must comply to appease the perceptual disturbance. As a result, employing techniques relevant to unique oneness theory alone may prove to be inadequate.

Having made this point, a combination of pharmacological therapy and unique oneness theory techniques to improve perceptual disturbances such as hallucinations is advantageous. Antipsychotic medications can ameliorate the intensity of the paranoid feelings and the hallucination, allowing a patient to recognize and comprehend the false nature of the perceptual disturbance. Nonpharmacological efforts can provide stability, while cognitive and behavioral techniques allow the patient to appreciate these misperceptions and more accurately assess true reality. In addition, these efforts may allow reduced dosages of medication therapies known to have significant side effects.

During relatively stable periods of functioning in a schizophrenic patient, unique oneness theory techniques may also provide a level of protection from exacerbations. Daily therapeutic exercises that provide positive feedback for accurate reality perception may serve as a preventative tool in avoiding deterioration. This serves two purposes by reducing other costly interventions and by empowering the individual with a degree of self-control.

Delusions and Disorganized Thought

The ability to coherently integrate information into a perceptual replica of reality is affected in most schizophrenic patients. Much of the time, the incoming sensory data about the external environment is misperceived through a lens of paranoia or altered emotional content. When internal images and voices are interjected into this replica, hallucinations result. But when the incoming images and voices from external stimuli are misperceived because of improperly functioning perceptual systems, delusions and disorganized thoughts are the main symptoms.

While hallucinations may be more difficult to control without pharmacological assistance, delusions and disorganized thoughts may be more amenable to nonpharmacological technique alone. This may be particularly true when symptoms are mild to moderate. Unique oneness theory offers a means by which an individual can understand why existing thought patterns are incongruent with reality testing. The discrepancy between these is then explained in terms of a faulty replication of the external reality internally, and the patient can begin to appreciate why his or her perception is in error.

These techniques may not avoid the need for medication assistance, but again, medication dose reduction and benefits in preventing relapses are strong considerations in applying unique oneness theory techniques as part of a therapeutic regimen.

Attention Deficit Hyperactivity Disorder

Over the last several decades, the number of both children and adults diagnosed with ADHD (attention deficit hyperactivity disorder) has grown significantly. The cause of ADHD isn't well defined since many social, genetic, and environmental theories exist in terms of causation. This disorder is included here to elucidate how unique oneness theory can have beneficial effects in disorders that may not be considered to have a primary perceptual problem. In reality, perceptual problems can manifest themselves in a variety of ways, and the same therapeutic techniques used for psychotic disorders may be helpful in these circumstances as well.

The main symptoms of ADHD include an inability to focus attention on task for prolonged periods of time, a degree of distractibility, motor restlessness, and a tendency toward impulsivity. Not all these features are necessarily present in a given patient, and a spectrum of severity exists among individuals as well. Though perceptions of reality and the environment are grossly intact, self-awareness of behavior and social interaction is impaired most of time. It is within this realm of self-perception where unique oneness theory can provide important treatments that alleviate behavioral problems and assist with improved social functioning.

Inattention and Distractibility

A key feature of ADHD is the inability to focus attention and stay on task for prolonged periods without suffering distractibility. Without question, this results in an internal difficulty in dealing with the attention skills to function normally. Many theories about causation of ADHD have to do with social and environmental influences that train the brain to jump from topic to topic. For example, the introduction of multitasking, ten-second television commercials, quick scan and deletion of tasks in e-mail inboxes, and many other modern-day influences have trained our brains to have short attention spans. By the same token, perceptual retraining can correct this problem to an extent.

By invoking unique oneness theory techniques, retraining people who have ADHD to appreciate feedback cues socially can help them self-monitor their focus. For example, defining a specific goal of a social interaction or a task can serve as a source of feedback support. Periodically, the person then assesses perceptually whether the goal is still at the center of his or her thoughts and actions or whether he or she has moved off task. By using perceptual feedback comparing reality to internal perception, the success or failure of attentional focus can be measured. In time, this serves as a tool to retrain a person with ADHD. The milder and the earlier such therapeutics are introduced, the more likely successful effects will be noticed.

Hyperactivity and Impulsivity

The inability to inhibit or suppress distraction mentally is similar to the inability to inhibit or suppress activity physically. Hyperactivity and impulsivity are simply the motor aspects of inattention. A patient with ADHD cannot remain still or relax without constant movement, or sometimes the person cannot refrain from acting in a situation where restraint would be socially appropriate. Again, this isn't a direct perceptual problem, but the techniques of unique oneness theory can assist in nonpharmacological treatment.

Consider a child with hyperactivity and impulsivity. He or she is unable to sit still at school and attend a lecture. As a result, the classroom is disrupted, the teacher becomes frustrated, and the child is unable to learn efficiently. By employing unique oneness theory techniques, the child can be taught specific perceptual cues to monitor so that internal and reality perceptions are more congruent. For example, the number of times a stereotyped movement occurs in a given period may signal poor hyperactivity control. This then can trigger the child to either invoke cognitive exercises or inform his or her parent that greater pharmacological control is needed.

The goal is to use unique oneness theory techniques to improve functioning and give an individual control. If the techniques themselves become a distraction, then clearly functioning will not be better. Individualization is using these therapeutic tools must be assessed to be sure optimal effects are being achieved.

Techniques Connecting Uniqueness and Oneness

In the examples of various disorders described, the application of unique oneness theory is relatively straightforward in how it can provide adjunctive tools for treatment. These techniques aren't intended to replace medications or other forms of treatment but simply to assist in the armamentarium of therapeutics available. This will allow not only new options of treatment but also a more holistic approach. Modern-day medicine, especially in westernized societies, often fails to incorporate global measures of care. Unique oneness theory seeks to change this trend.

In addition to some of the techniques mentioned in these specific disorders, some general techniques that enhance our perceptual health can be used, even when medical disorders aren't present. By providing a link between the external world and our internal consciousness, a more accurate perception of reality can evolve. Creativity and likely a wide range of physical and mental health advantages occur when we explore these types of techniques.

Techniques that allow an expansion of our mental perceptions include activities such as meditation, relaxation techniques, breathing exercises, and prayer. The key role of each of these exercises is to reduce the amount of external stimuli and allow greater perception of internal awareness. In the process, a deeper consciousness evolves, invoking universal connections with the oneness of reality. While direct sensory stimuli trigger our mental perceptions of the world around us, and while preexisting memories influence the interpretation of this data, deep connections with our inner consciousness enable access to the one true reality that exists beyond our individual existence. No matter what exercises we pursue, our perceptions will always carry individual uniqueness. But the more time we spend connecting to our inner consciousness, the more we become unified with the universe and gain a more accurate perception of the one true reality.

As we move from child to adult, we tend to place greater importance on the external world and its sensory stimuli. In other words, we rely on mental perceptions of a concrete world based on objective data. Our memories and experiences shape our interpretations of this data, and our unique perceptions move further away from the oneness of the universe. We slowly become slaves to our brains and the secondary information they provide us in determining reality perceptions.

But as a child, we were likely more creative and imaginative. The use of daydreaming as a technique was naturally employed in augmenting this creative and internal state of reality perception. As adults, we tend to place less importance on such activities as we become more attentive to the external world. But in a daydreaming state, the boundaries between internal, and external worlds are less distinct. A blending between objective stimuli and subjective imagination occurs, enabling uniqueness and oneness to coexist. Daydreaming is, in fact, an ideal way to promote greater perceptual health.

I imagine Bill Gates and Steve Jobs are some people in the world today who regularly practice such activities as daydreaming. In fact, they may not even realize its importance in their lives or their creative process. Daydreaming bridges the gap in reality perception between what we actually perceive with our physical and mental senses and what we can intuitively perceive through our internal consciousness. Just like meditation, music, and even biofeedback techniques provide a heightened state of awareness, daydreaming enhances perception of not only objective signals but also internal subjective ones. This ultimately creates a more accurate perspective of our environment and universe.

Anyone can practice daydreaming exercises. The more passionate we are about something, the easier it is. Initially set aside ten to fifteen minutes a day when you simply let your mind daydream about any subject you like. Don't let the worries and anxieties of the day creep into this time but instead allow your thoughts and emotions to travel in a direction of fantasy and creativity. Your need to anchor these daydreams in some degree of objective reality will naturally occur, so this need not be a concern. Simply focus on your internal dreams and passions, and lose yourself for the period you have.

By employing this technique of daydreaming daily and by gradually lengthening the time, you will progressively gain more expansive and accurate perceptual abilities into your daily life. This will allow you to perceive reality from new perspectives and gain greater personal insights. In addition, the benefits to your physical and mental health are likely to be significant as a result. These are indeed areas where greater validation through research needs to occur, but significant data already support the benefits of similar techniques on our health.

Conclusion

The ability to educate patients about internal perception and the creation of a replica of the external environment gives them a sense of understanding and control over some of their symptoms.

This degree of empowerment is important because it allows them to be active participants in their care. Medication, which is certainly a necessary treatment in most cases, provides a passive means by which a disorder is controlled. But combining both measures likely will provide the best effect in achieving treatment success and in avoiding negative effects.

As previously mentioned, these types of nonpharmacological interventions have been shown to have objective benefits in treatment of diseases. Research to support this has been scant to date, and certainly more directed research would be helpful. In the chapters to follow, the mechanisms by which unique oneness theory affects perception and disease states will be suggested as will potential areas for future research. Through this, stronger evidence can support how nonpharmacological treatments, such as those outlined here, affect health and illness.

Direct and indirect methods of intervention can be employed that use unique oneness theory concepts. Individual disease states as well as individuals themselves will determine to what extent each of these will be helpful. These techniques may have the greatest impact in known perceptual disease states, but even mild disorders such as personality dysfunctions, social phobias, and other minor psychological disturbances stand to benefit from these techniques. Through gaining a better understanding of the perceptual processes of the brain and their relationship to consciousness, new doors for therapeutics will undoubtedly be unlocked.

Applications of Unique Oneness Theory

B y understanding the premises of unique oneness theory, we embrace the notice of one ultimate reality as well as numerous individual perceptions. In addition, we also accept that variations of perceived reality can fall along a spectrum that ranges from normal and socially acceptable to abnormal and socially deviant or pathological. Thus far, we have seen how specific perceptual disturbances can account for human symptomatology in a variety of disorders. Hence, we will consider a more general application of unique oneness theory principles in developing and expanding techniques of therapy and research.

The overriding principles that govern today's understanding of human behavior stem from a cause-and-effect type of perspective. In other words, an environmental stimulus occurs and triggers a reaction in human behavior. The death of a loved one causes sadness and grief. A deficiency in a specific brain chemical creates an imbalance in function and triggers symptoms. But what if this perspective was an oversimplification and held a very limited view of human behavior? What if human behavior was, in fact, more dynamic and interactive rather than simply a cause-and-effect scenario?

Unique oneness theory supports such a complex interaction in describing behavior. The environment indeed provides stimuli, resulting in human perceptions and eventually behaviors, but additionally human behavior can exert an impact and influence on how perceptions are viewed and interpreted. These influences can be either conscious or unconscious. In other words, a dynamic interaction between the environment and the perceptual system determines a final perception of reality.

For example, the predetermined response of a warrior to suppress pain awareness is often characterized in modern-day cinema and is well recognized. This represents a conscious awareness in changing the perception of a pain stimulus. In contrast, the perception that a placebo results in amelioration of symptoms is an unconscious, or at least less conscious, manipulation of perception and reaction. This demonstrates that we have some degree of control over perception. In turn, we also influence our behavioral response secondarily. We can influence human behavior through our perceptual systems rather than simply through rational systems of cognitive logic.

In this chapter, we will examine how different techniques in psychotherapy can use this information to alter their techniques and achieve greater efficacy in their result. Further different types of psychotherapy can incorporate greater perceptual aspects of focus under their theoretical realms. In turn, this will broaden their ability to alter pathological behavior and create greater well-being.

Additionally, these same principles of understanding can be applied to pharmacology. When we gain a better perspective in neuroplasticity, specific neurotransmitter systems, and regional brain functions as they pertain to perception, we learn that medications can assist in promoting positive behavioral change. Medications may promote greater perceptual control for individuals or provide greater awareness of perceptions in relation to ultimate reality. Both would have advantages in promoting better health through perceptual systems.

Finally, understanding the implications of unique oneness theory in regard to modern medicine can enable new directions of research. This will likely lead to different methods of therapy and medication treatments, which have demonstrated objective benefit, but criteria for studying such benefits must first be standardized and developed. Invoking standards for behavioral measurements must continue to advance. In addition, consideration of intangible and less objective aspects of science must be looked at. Opening our eyes to nonmaterial influences on human behavior and disease can allow new insights in medicine to occur. Appreciating concepts of entanglement, universal reciprocity, and psychokinetic energies warrant greater investigation through traditional and possible newly acquired scientific techniques.

Unique Oneness Theory and Psychotherapy Considerations

While many subcategories of psychotherapy are available and practiced on a regular basis, the primary focus of this section will deal with the three primary schools of psychotherapy techniques existing in the medical world today. Most forms of psychotherapy fall under psychoanalytic techniques, cognitive behavioral therapy techniques, or humanistic-existential techniques. To a degree, all incorporate perceptual abilities into their strategies of therapy, but this aspect will be considered in greater detail since it pertains to unique oneness theory.

To a significant degree, a correlation exists between one's thoughts and the ability to embrace unique oneness. In other words, the more in sync a person's thoughts are in relation to his or her own personal uniqueness and the oneness of reality, the greater is his or her ability to maintain good physical and mental health. If the correlation is poor, health disorders become evident; but if the correlation is higher, proper functioning is enjoyed. This is the basic concept in employing unique oneness theory within different forms of therapy and treatment.

In a schizophrenic state, for example, the disorganized thinking that occurs is caused from a loss of correlation between one's thoughts and the unique oneness of reality for that person. If therapy or treatment can align thoughts to a greater extent with unique oneness, then clinical improvement will occur. In theory, it should be possible to mathematically determine the degree of correlation between thoughts and unique oneness perceptions in various disorders. The same would also apply to individuals suffering from physical ailments secondary to a mental detachment from unique oneness perceptual abilities.

In this regard, an Alzheimer's patient would likely suffer a high loss of correlation between thoughts and unique oneness perceptions, while a highly functioning individual in society would have a strong correlation between the two. Any condition where one identified more strongly with his or her thoughts in determining a perception of reality would have the potential to result in a decline of function and possibly in developing a health disorder. Anxiety states, phobias, substance abuse, alcohol abuse, and even brain trauma all reflect this type of situation.

One may suspect we are dealing with a chicken-and-the-egg phenomenon here. The loss of correlation could be assumed to simply be the consequence of the disease state rather than a factor in its development. Certainly, this has been traditional medicine's viewpoint through the years. However, unique oneness theory supports the loss of correlation as an etiologic factor in causing both mental and physical disease states. Similarly, it also supports that it can play a role in treating such conditions.

Over time, individuals can create a universal illusion that all the reality exists outside their inner existence. External objects create the only reality for these individuals without any consideration for a true universal reality, an inner conscious state, or the unique influences that affect their thoughts and objective perceptions. This external focus results in a perceptual illusion that prevents unique oneness phenomena from being appreciated as they lie hidden from awareness. These individuals are unable to acknowledge the existence of anything else other than what they can objectively sense. Over time, the lack of contact with the oneness of the universe and a more accurate perception of true reality weakens the brain and body. This ultimately can cause a variety of poor health conditions.

The goal is therefore to realign a person's unique perception closer to the one true reality as described by unique oneness theory. This occurs through appreciating that perceived reality is composed not only of objective stimuli but also of innate memories, past experiences, and a connection to universal reality. Through understanding this and expanding perceptual abilities to include deeper consciousness, a higher degree of correlation between mind, body, and reality can occur. In turn, better mental, emotional, and physical health can be realized. With this in mind, specific therapy techniques will now be considered in pursuing these therapeutic goals.

Psychoanalytic Theory

Introduced originally by Sigmund Freud, psychoanalytic theory is based on theories introduced in the mid-twentieth century containing components of Darwinism and the extent of medical knowledge at the time. Though psychoanalysis theory has changed through the decades, the basis still holds that human personality develops through the interaction of three main psychic domains, known as the id, the ego, and the superego.

The id represents base human desires seeking to influence behavior through the pain and pleasure principle, while the superego holds ethical and moral concepts that influence behavior through what is valued in a society. These personality aspects are important, but the ego is the key component that deals with reality and the ultimate output of behavior after considering input from the id and superego. Ego is believed to be where perceptual interpretations and influences are made.

In addition to these three components of human personality development, the other key features of psychoanalytic theory define three domains of human awareness. These include the conscious, the preconscious, and the subconscious. The conscious is our overt awareness of what we perceive as reality, while the subconscious lies beneath our level of awareness and is inaccessible for routine retrieval. The preconscious, however, is a reservoir of information and memories, which can be brought into the conscious realm. It is here that our unique perceptions of reality may be influenced in a dynamic sense to affect behavior according to psychoanalytic theory.

In traditional psychoanalysis, a patient verbally expresses his or her thoughts, which include not only conscious thoughts but also preconscious thoughts. For example, free associations, fantasies, and other emotions are described along with memories. By accessing conscious and preconscious perceptions, the therapist can determine or uncover subconscious conflicts. Dream content, which is thought to represent subconscious conflicts as well, can also be used in this form of therapy. Since conscious awareness and the ego determine the patient's behavior, bringing greater awareness of preconscious and subconscious conflicts secondarily allows a change in human behavior.

For instance, if a person has suppressed subconscious anger toward an abusive parent, the conflict between the superego's value of loving one's parent and the id's need to avoid pain may create ego disturbances in behavior. This conflict may perpetuate into adulthood and manifest itself in other relationship and behaviors. By identifying these conflicts and bringing them into a conscious realm, the ego is then able to incorporate this new conscious information and change the way the person behaves. The same environmental trigger that caused one's aberrant behavior before can now result in a different (and presumably better) behavior after the subconscious conflict is identified.

In psychoanalytic theory, the acknowledgment that one ultimate reality exists and that unique individual perceptions affect consciousness can be easily incorporated into both theory and practice. Subconscious conflicts can drive inaccurate perceptions of reality. Preconscious suppressed memories and thoughts can likewise influence how reality is perceived. Providing alternative perceptions of the true reality in the context of personality development and behavior is a means by which unique oneness theory can provide additional benefits in psychoanalytic techniques. And these can subsequently be used at a conscious level to promote more accurate reality perceptions.

When we embrace the fact that the ego can alter reality perception through changing its extent of consciousness, we see it is intuitive that a dynamic relationship between the ego's perceptual abilities and environmental realities exists. One doesn't trigger the other in only a cause-and-effect phenomenon, but instead an interactive process ensues by which both reality and perception can alter a behavioral response. Thus, passive perception of environmental stimuli and active perceptions, guided by the ego's influence, combine to produce the final behavioral result. Unique oneness theory is therefore quite complimentary to psychoanalytic theories and techniques.

Cognitive Behavioral Therapy and Unique Oneness Theory

Cognitive behavioral therapies (CBT) are more difficult to specify than other forms of therapy, since these have become a catchall for many different approaches. The blending of cognitive and behavioral therapies form the origin of this category of psychotherapeutic care, and as a result a wide range of procedures have become accepted under its umbrella. For the purpose of this section, a relatively simplistic definition will be used. CBT will be defined as any therapy that seeks to define and change underlying thoughts and emotions that result together in generating unwanted social behaviors.

Notably this definition is broad, but likewise so is the range of disorders for which CBT is used. Mood disorders, personality disorders, behavioral disturbances, substance abuse problems, and psychotic dysfunctions are all categories of illness where CBT plays an active role in therapy. The goal in each case is to identify the underlying thought disturbance and/or emotion that supports the behaviors and then alters this pattern of thought and/or emotion to achieve different behavioral results. Sometimes this is performed through traditional algorithms and sometimes simply by rational trial and error. As a result, the scope of therapy under CBT can cover many areas.

When applying unique oneness theory to CBT, the most important aspect is correlating emotions and thoughts to the unique perceptions of an individual's experiences. Reality is fixed and uniform, so changing reality to alter behavior is not a feature of unique oneness theory or CBT. Therefore, both share an approach at identifying underlying mechanisms that explain reality as a means to alter human behavior. Unique oneness theory approaches this through perceptual means as it relates to consciousness and awareness, while CBT approaches this only through thoughts and emotions.

The interesting point here is that thoughts and emotions are based on perceptual impressions of reality. In CBT, the ability to change patterns of thoughts or emotions is often the goal to attain a different behavioral outcome. It makes reasonable sense, then, that changing perceptions, which underlie thoughts and feelings, is another means by which behavior can be effectively changed. In fact, many cognitive behavioral therapists suggest a perceptual alternative to change patterns of thought, emotion, and behavior.

For example, in a social phobia disorder, a person may be afraid to be in public places or among large crowds. The unique perception of being amid many people may be uncomfortable, causing feelings of fear, anxiety, and tension. Thoughts of impending doom may develop if the reaction is severe enough. In reality, there is no immediate danger, but the person's unique perception of the situation states otherwise. Using CBT, the thoughts and emotions of the situation are defined and shown to be inconsistent with logical thought. But at the same time, unique oneness theory could demonstrate the perceptual errors in the situation's assessment and seek to change the perception at the root level. In this manner, unique oneness theory and CBT could be used concomitantly to attain positive results.

Depending on the underlying problem, unique oneness theory and CBT can be combined in different fashions to accomplish the optimal benefits to the patient. In some cases, such as psychotic disorders, unique oneness theory, CBT, and pharmacological measures may all be used to achieve a complimentary effect. The important key in this situation is to add a degree of perceptual control to the techniques of CBT that employ thought and emotional control. The added focus on perception not only provides another tool for the patient to use for changing his or her behavior but also facilitates a change in maladaptive thoughts and emotions regardless of the cause.

Unique Oneness Theory and Humanistic Therapies

Humanistic therapies, like other forms of psychotherapy, have evolved over several decades. The basic essence of humanistic psychological therapies is founded on existentialism. Its focus is primarily on human interactions and experiences as being the source of positive behavioral change. In other words, people have power to alter their course through self-actualization and self-empowerment, which manifest themselves during human experience in life. Perhaps because of this, unique oneness theory and its attention on perceptual control offer the greatest benefit under this rubric of psychotherapy.

The central focus in humanistic therapy is on the individual. Attention is directed more toward the positive attributes and strengths of an individual rather than on the pathological problem. This allows a patient to develop a stronger sense of self and overcome pathological or aberrant aspects of his or her personality or character. Through intensive one-on-one dialogue with the therapist, self-actualization gradually occurs as these positive attributes are highlighted.

Compared to psychoanalytic and cognitive behavior therapies, humanistic therapies are most concerned with human experience in reality and in awarding meaning to the human experience. If psychoanalysis and CBT focus on the inner working of the mind and psyche, humanistic therapies have a more outward perspective, combining human characteristics of an individual with happenings in an individual's life. Therefore, perception of reality plays a significant role in determining the extent of self-actualization and positive changes in behaviors.

In applying unique oneness theory to humanistic forms of psychotherapy, the most congruent method in combining the two would be to focus on an optimistic view of reality perception. This doesn't imply a perception that distorts reality to a favorable extent. Reality should remain truthful to its monistic view. However, shifting a perspective of perception from one that contains negative conceptions to one that is more positive would be both effective in changing behaviors and consistent with humanistic theory. The perception encouraged would highlight the individual's strengths and assets.

For example, in a situation where a marital argument ensues, an individual with known tendencies toward depression and self-sacrificing characteristics perceives the cause of the argument as being his or her fault. In turn, guilt is felt, and behaviors are geared toward trying to appease the situation through further self-sacrificial means. The eventual behavior results from a distorted perception of the argument as emanating from personal faults.

When we use unique oneness theory in combination with humanistic therapy, the goal would be to alter the perception of the argument in a direction more positive. The expressions the patient would have during the argument could be perceived as personal strength and as being honest with his or her wife. In a similar fashion, real yet positive aspects of the event could be discussed, providing a more favorable perception of the overall argument. This empowers the patient to see the good behaviors amid the bad simply by changing his or her unique perception of reality.

Many humanistic therapists may actually already employ techniques that attempt perceptual control in assessing personal life experience. If so, then the concepts of unique oneness theory are already ingrained in one's techniques. In essence, the therapist is simply guiding the patient toward a more positive, unique perception of reality, which allows better reactions and behaviors. This, is turn, according to humanistic theory, adds meaning and value to a person's life and begins to shape behaviors into a progressively more meaningful life direction.

Unique Oneness Theory and Pharmacological Considerations

When it comes to the study of perception, pharmacological research has primarily involved the study of hallucinogenic effects on the brain. Since Albert Hofmann discovered LSD in 1943, the ability of chemical substances to influence reality perception has been intriguing. Since that time, many other hallucinogenic substances have been discovered, and the common finding among them all has been their effect on the serotonin neurotransmitter system.

Specifically, the serotonin receptor in the brain, called 5HT-2A, seems to be the most commonly affected structure when it comes to hallucinogens. This serotonin receptor is concentrated in the fifth layer of our brain's cortex (layer V) and plays a significant role in coordinating perceptual activity. The neurons of this layer receive sensory input from all areas of the nervous system and then relay the information to deeper brain structures and other cortical areas. This distribution of information provides cohesion of sensory experience that is realized by multiple nervous system structures and accounts for our unique perception of reality at any given time.

This cohesion of information is known as sensory binding. Sensory binding allows us to perceive visual stimuli, tactile stimuli, auditory stimuli, and more simultaneously in multiple brain regions, creating a holistic experience. If a hallucinogenic substance is introduced, there is a destabilization of this cohesion. The result is distortion in various perceptions, whether visual, auditory, or others, which we know as psychedelic hallucinations. In a similar manner, psychotic perceptual disturbances in schizophrenia and other psychiatric disorders may involve similar destabilizing mechanisms.

While pharmacology has suggested serotonin receptors as being pertinent in perceptual disturbances, dopamine has also been suggested. The reasons for this include the fact that schizophrenic patients tend to have a greater number of dopamine receptors than healthy subjects; anti-dopamine medications reduce perceptual disturbances in schizophrenic patients over time; and dopamine is an excitatory neurotransmitter involved in multiple systems in the brain. Therefore, trying to sort out the significance between 5HT-2A receptors and dopamine receptors in perceptual neurochemistry has been difficult, to say the least. Debate still exists over the importance of both neurotransmitters.

Regardless of the debate, it's clear that reality perception can be affected in a negative fashion by both chemicals and disease. However, improvements in individual perceptions can also be accomplished through medications. This concept supports that the use of pharmacology in creating more accurate perceptions of reality is and should be a focus for efforts in addressing various psychological disturbances. Using effective medications that promote greater accuracy in perception can only help other psychological techniques.

The interplay between the cortical serotonin neuron projections and the subthalamic dopamine neuron projections seem to both interact with a very important deep brain structure, the thalamus. The thalamus is involved in many aspects related to alertness and awareness. In fact, many experts who believe in brain-related theories of awareness feel the thalamus is the seat of consciousness. The interactions between serotonin and dopamine with the thalamus may indeed be where multiple environmental stimuli are integrated in developing unique perceptions for the individual. Targeting these neural pathways and their neurotransmitters makes logical sense for future pursuits in perceptual pharmacology.

Another interesting aspect pharmacological research has suggested has been the concepts of neurotoxicity and neuroplasticity. Neurotoxicity describes the injury to neurons and other cell structures that result from chemical effects and their toxins. Neuroplasticity, on the other hand, refers to the ability of neurons and their networks of connections to adapt and change to different inputs and environments. Both have been suggested as mechanisms in causing permanent effects from hallucinogenic drugs.

Hallucinogen persistent perceptual disorder (HPPD) is a chronic condition that can develop after prolonged psychedelic drug use. Mescaline, LSD, and psilocybin have all been associated with this condition. HPPD can present a range of aberrant perceptual symptoms, but the main key is that all are characterized by persistent distortions in the perception of reality. The most enduring theory is that these drugs cause chemical injury to nerve cells, resulting in an inability to function normally. Instead of suppressing unwanted perceptions and augmenting ones that coincide with reality, a maximum of perceptions (both real and unreal) exists simultaneously.

However, neuroplasticity offers another perspective on why these perceptual disturbances may exist. In this scenario, the effects of the psychedelic drugs alter the normal physiology of perceptual processing in the brain. Connections among neurons that wouldn't normally be excited by reality stimuli are stimulated through chemical means. As a result, these networks are enhanced because they are being used more often than normal. Eventually, these nerve networks become more extensive and begin to augment aberrant perceptions, even when the drug stimulation is no longer present. This is the mechanism in which neuroplasticity may play a role.

While the purpose of this section isn't to determine which theory is more accurate, the interesting fact about these current pharmacological views regarding perception is that medications and chemicals can indeed influence unique individual perceptions of reality. Certainly, we have more knowledge of how hallucinogens cause dysfunction than we do regarding beneficial effects. But this does demonstrate the potential for their use in altering individual perceptions to coincide more closely with the one true reality.

These findings are also important in supporting the underlying beliefs of unique oneness theory. The integration of environmental stimuli and its vulnerability to chemical influence provides an explanation how unique individual perceptions of reality occur. Through normal physiology, neuroplasticity can provide alterations of perceptual integrations based on each individual's unique life experience. No two people have the same life experience, and thus their perception of reality is inherently going to be different at a neurological level. If this is the case, then certainly continued efforts in finding effective pharmacological agents to manipulate individual perceptions can open doors of opportunity in treating medical illness.

Research Considerations Regarding Unique Oneness Theory

As discussed, the need for research regarding new pharmacological agents in relationship to perceptual systems is apparent. Likewise, investigating the use of different psychotherapy techniques using unique oneness theory concepts and perceptual control can benefit future directions of health care. Readdressing these issues again here isn't warranted. Instead, two important points need to be made regarding directions of future research as they pertain to perceptual processing and aberrancies.

The first consideration isn't anything new. Human behavior is certainly complex, and many variables are involved when considering integrated relationships. Whenever a new variable is introduced into a situation, the resulting change is difficult to associate directly into a cause-and-effect relationship. The reason for this is simply that one variable rarely has an isolated effect on change. Multiple effects often ensue, and the result is a complex array of all these effects and the preexisting condition. No matter how well controlled an experiment may be, these complexities and multiple interactions limit research abilities.

Now that I have said this, we can see that steps to try to standardize research methods in assessing human behaviors have been ongoing. Continuing these efforts will be increasingly important as we explore the effect of unique individual perceptions of reality on human behaviors. While one's individual perception greatly influences the eventual reaction on the part of a person, many variables are present. Mood, memories, thought patterns, education level, gender, cultural biases, and many other factors affect unique perceptions. Just as in pharmacology research, where the exact mechanism of action can be difficult to define despite a beneficial response, identifying which unique factor affects one's perception to the greatest extent can be a challenge.

The hope of establishing a complete standard by which human perception can be analyzed may never occur; but with each step toward greater objective measurements of behavior and perceptual change, the degree of influence unique perceptions have in relating to human behavior and dysfunction can be determined to a greater extent. This, in turn, will lead to more targeted approaches to treatment and therapy, whether through medications or psychotherapy techniques. In addition to realizing that perceptual differences account in part for behavior variances, we must also accept the challenge to develop standards in measuring these differences more accurately.

The second area of medical research highlighted by unique oneness theory is the investigation of nonmaterial influences on the human body and its perceptual mechanisms. As shown in other chapters of this book, phenomena that cannot be currently explained by material associations aren't uncommon. Experiments that seem to indicate psychic energy affecting results have been reported. Associations of some material entities persist, even when they are no longer near with one another. And seemingly, objects share reciprocity with other objects, universally suggesting a constant degree of connectedness.

Studies and reports have been provided that suggest the presence of these nonmaterial influences, but admittedly they are limited. This fact doesn't nullify their existence, but it does perpetuate a lack of understanding and possibly a closed door into the next important phase of discovery in medicine. If indeed nothingness or space is occupied by a force not able to be perceived by current human abilities, its influence on things we can measure would escape detection. Some philosophers suspect this nothingness is the real source of human consciousness. Perhaps it is. It takes only a moment to consider that vast unoccupied space that exists in every molecule of our bodies to understand this could have significant implications. This would influence not only medicine but also all science.

Applying this possibility to science in general would open new doors for the future and create a mechanism by which entanglement and reciprocity could be explained. It would provide a means by which psychic energy could influence matter and health. Whether we are open to such possibilities is pointless if we never choose to examine such a presence. Research must begin to develop new means by which nonmaterial influences on health can be assessed. Failure to do so will continue to hinder progress in many scientific fields. Of these, psychology and psychiatry are among the most vulnerable.

According to unique oneness theory, a monistic true reality exists for everyone, regardless of our unique differences and less-than-perfect perceptions. It is intuitive that such a reality must have a common origination with our own human existence. Whether one believes in a supernatural being or a big bang theory, this association is apparent. It isn't so farfetched to consider some force linking everything in the universe together, since one may exist. This would be the same force that created a single reality we each perceive and account for usual phenomenon that escapes current logic.

For medicine to reach new heights in discovery, a willingness to embrace the illogical and unknown must be present. Creating better research methods to explore such untraditional hypotheses is important for us to begin to explain human diseases and disorders more fully. The potential this holds for our future as human beings is truly incomprehensible.

Beyond Medicine

Unique oneness theory pleads for a paradigm shift to occur in the way we think about the human mind and body. Traditional westernized medicine continues to have its foundations in principles that isolate cause and effect in a direct and singular relationship. In this regard, a shift toward a perspective that supports dynamic, complex, and integrated explanations for medical occurrences is needed. In doing so, we will begin to see new relationships that were otherwise not possible.

In addition, a paradigm shift needs to occur in the way disease and health are envisioned. Greater openness to new ideas and less resistance to change must be present for this to happen on a large scale. But medicine isn't the only area where such change is needed. In fact, paradigm shifts that have affected medicine over the centuries have typically resulted in major changes in world views as well.

For example, at the beginning of the book, the discoveries and opinions of Galileo and Copernicus completely changed how the word viewed the galaxy. Man was no longer egocentric and the center of the universe. Instead the sum was the center of the galaxy, and mankind simply existed within this new structure. This change had repercussions on the psyche of humankind well outside the realm of astronomy. Likewise, the discovery of bacteria, which were never before seen with the naked eye, created a major shift in the way disease was explained. Witches, punishments for sins, and a variety of other explanations fell by the wayside as microbiology stepped onto the scene. Widespread effects in human behavior resulted from this single discovery.

Darwinism, the discovery of DNA, psychoanalytic theory, and many other new perspectives have resulted in similar shifts not only in medicine but also in world views. Here the facets of unique oneness theory hold the same potential. If new views of consciousness, perception, and self are adopted for the sake of scientific exploration, the discoveries that may be found could have the power to once again change the world. Attention to energies and intangible forces in relationship to disease may pave the way for new perspectives, even outside the world of medicine.

Areas that may be affected could include environmental science, technology, communications, philosophy and religion, physics, and many others. Imagine understanding how one action on the other side of the world impacts another seemingly unrelated change elsewhere. Consider Western and Eastern medicines and beliefs merging into one holistic perspective. These are the considerations that will be explored in the subsequent chapter as it pertains to unique oneness theory and how global effects of this paradigm shift might be realized.

CHAPTER 11

A Truly Unifying Application

Dichotomies exist all around us. The objective contrasts with the subjective. Light and dark struggle against one another. Good and evil are long-time philosophical opponents. When we consider perception, such dichotomies are no different. In fact, through a better understanding of perceptual capacity, various dualities can be better understood. especially regarding reality. Like most dualistic concepts, extremes cannot exist without its counterpart, and polar perceptual components demonstrate the same degree of connectedness.

Unique oneness theory has been shown to embrace both the objective and subjective sides of perception. In doing so, a grasp of how our world and experiences are perceived can be better understood from a holistic perceptive. Science and physics don't need to represent a completely separate field of study from philosophy and religion. Both fields of interest have common ground just as subjective and objective aspects of reality do. One doesn't survive without the other despite apparent differences in beliefs.

As a final review and an attempt to define both current and future applications for unique oneness theory, this chapter will cohesively integrate the concepts discussed in the book thus far and offer some thoughts to ponder for future considerations. We stand at the threshold now more than ever of understanding the links between the mind, body, consciousness, and reality. A paradigm shift in how we view such concepts may finally allow us to make Albert Einstein's lifelong dream of a unification of all fields of human study a reality. Unique oneness theory hopes to be a major step in that direction.

Review of External and Internal Realities

Perception essentially requires two integral parts. One is the existence of external reality, and the other is a creation of an internal reality. External reality consists of objective components of our universe and experiences. For example, an automobile we drive has specific objective characteristics we can measure. It's made of carbon fiber and steel, which have specific densities and weights. It harbors an engine that uses combustible fuels and/or electricity. It occupies space and dimensions according to its specific type of matter. All these features can be objectively measured according to Newtonian laws of physics and other basic laws of science.

However, external reality also has subjective components. The same automobile may have all the above features that are easily defined, but predicting how the automobile will travel along a road or behave during an impact is much more difficult. A seemingly infinite number of possibilities of behavior exist, depending on a variety of variables, and defining this part of external reality has led to the field of quantum physics. Though some aspects of quantum physics remain in question, the basic essence of quantum physics and quantum mechanics is to capture the subjective aspect of external realities. These theories provide a mathematical framework to explain the multiple possibilities in which atoms and molecules may behave, given a specific set of circumstances.

Therefore, external reality, as the law of science today defines it, clearly has objective and subjective components. A duality and often a dichotomy are present when trying to explain the true nature or external reality in the universe. Yet neither the objective nor subjective is more important than the other. Both are present and needed to completely explain what is believed to be true reality. As stated several times through the course of this book, unique oneness theory holds that a true reality indeed exists and is the basis for all human perception. External reality is the ultimate experiential reality from which subsequent perception proceeds.

Internal reality, on the other hand, is the reality we carry within us. Like external reality, internal reality also has objective and subjective components. Our bodies, our physical brains, neurochemical processes, and the physical components of our sensory processing comprise the objective aspects of our internal reality. For example, we internally realize the automobile traveling down the road as our eyes see the object, connect to memory and interpretative areas of our brains, and enable the internal representation of symbol mentally. These physical and chemical processes are internally no different from the physical and scientific phenomena described previously within external reality. Both are objective and can be measured.

However, this objective aspect of internal reality would have little meaning without its subjective counterpart. The subjective components of self-awareness and consciousness add flavor and meaning to internal realities. It is one thing to create internal mental images and symbols from sensory stimuli but quite another to assign meaning to these symbols, which extend beyond concrete objective definitions. Awareness of self and consciousness makes each of us unique while simultaneously linking us with every other thing in the universe. In other words, subjective aspects provide uniqueness, while objective aspects provide unity.

To summarize, reality is therefore composed of dual aspects for each of us. A fixed external reality provides an absolute framework, on which true reality is based. This explains why exact laws of science are so rigid. Without a fixed and absolute external world, on which to base perception, inherent errors would exist and prevent the needed unification and stability of our universe. In addition, we each have an internal reality that interacts, interprets, and analyzes the external reality through objective and subjective levels of processing. The internal reality thus introduces individual uniqueness in how we perceive the fixed external reality. At a very basic level, these are the building blocks on which unique oneness theory is based.

Review of Perceptual Ability

Now that we have rediscussed external and internal realities, perception can be more easily understood. The uniformity and oneness of external reality interact with the uniqueness of individual internal realities to create a unique perception, through which each of us experiences life. Once again, a duality exists within the realm of perception, just as it does for external and internal reality. Both oneness and uniqueness are essential components.

Perceptual ability, however, requires a congruency between external and internal reality. In other words, the key must fit the lock to open the door to accurate perception. If aberrancies and mismatches exist between the two, faulty perception occurs, leading to a variety of perceptual disorders. These have been covered in part under the pathological medical conditions described in this book, but perceptual disturbances aren't limited to only medical diseases.

Routine and common perceptual mismatches occur daily and can lead to disagreements, differences of opinion, poor decisions, and many other behaviors considered nonpathological in nature. The bottom line is that the more accurate internal reality matches external reality, the more accurate perception will be.

Consider for a moment this medical example. LSD is a known hallucinatory drug that causes severe alterations of perception. The most accepted mechanism of action by which LSD causes these effects is through blocking norepinephrine receptors in the brain. Because the correct neurotransmitter cannot access its normal nerve receptor, a distorted or altered interpretation of external reality occurs. This is the basis of LSD-induced hallucinations. Because the LSD-influenced internal reality (resulting in an inability for accurate neurotransmitter-receptor connections) doesn't match external reality (the fixed true reality), perception is flawed, resulting in transient pathology. The lack of congruency between these two systems causes inaccurate perception.

The internal mind-brain complex must be able to create a perception of the external reality that is nearly identical to the real thing. This is a premise of unique oneness theory. An internal replica of our universe must be devised through sensory phenomena for subjective experiences, feeling, emotions, and even meaning to give relevance to our individual and collective experience in life. But more importantly, the inability to approximate true reality leads to altered perceptions and perceptual disorders regardless of the cause. Whether trauma, chemical imbalances, or simply altered logic is the cause of the dichotomy, the result is perceptual distortion and poorly adaptive functioning within the universe.

Because we understand this concept of unique oneness theory as it pertains to perception, a greater understanding of a variety of altered mind-body and objective-subjective dichotomies can be gained. Disorders that cause objective disturbances of internal reality processes result in perceptual problems. This has been described previously through examples such as schizophrenia, Alzheimer's dementia, and other psychoses. Likewise, disorders of self-awareness and consciousness can result in the same incongruence and dichotomy, rendering the same effect. The focus here will always be on internal reality. since external reality is fixed and uniform. And while altered internal reality explains a great deal about altered perception, altering internal reality through various mechanisms offers hope for treating misperceptions.

Opportunities for changing altered internal realities can come from many different areas. Medicines and surgeries have traditionally offered remedies in Western societies. Herbal therapies, meditation, and biofeedback have been more readily accepted by Eastern cultures. Truly, both approaches provide means by which more accurate reality perception can occur, and limiting our approach to optimal health to only one of these is certainly shortsighted. Just as the gap between science and philosophy should be erased, so should be the dichotomy between Eastern and Western medical approaches.

Death: The Ultimate Perceptual Disorder

Does death truly occur? Before answering the question with an assured affirmative response, for a moment consider the dichotomies we are discussing. From the perspective of external reality, we witness death all the time. People age and succumb to death throughout our lifetimes. Plants and animals come and go. Just as birth and life occur, death is guaranteed to soon follow given certain circumstances and/or an allowance of time. It would therefore appear that indeed death is a perceptual reality.

However, the aspect of death we see is that of physical death. When the decay of matter occurs over time, this eventually results in an absence of life from that form. When we continue our discussion of dichotomies, it would be responsible to state that the body depends on the power of life to exist. Without life, the body is dead. It's the relationship between a substance and its attributes that is integrally related yet specifically distinct. In other words, a duality between the two is present and is required to yield a living body. Consider a red rose as another example. The substance of the rose itself is its objective form of matter. Its red color is simply an attribute of the rose. The two are integrally related, and at the same time. both imply meaning to the whole. A yellow rose is distinctly different from a red rose. It contains a different attribute to its objective form.

Understand that the body and life are both required to yield a living body. What exactly happens when death takes over and life ceases to exist within that body? From a physical perspective, the body is considered dead. The heart no longer beats, the lungs no longer expand, and brain activity goes silent. But the inner consciousness and life that once occupied that body still remain within the universe. They may no longer exist within the actual body, which lies dead before us, but it persists nonetheless. The relationship between these two components has been severed, leading us to the perception that death of a person (or other living form) has occurred. However, the more accurate perception may be that the duality between life and form has separated and that the life energy has gone elsewhere.

According to the laws of physics, energy can be neither created nor destroyed. While the matter of the physical body decays after death, it remains in a material form. Likewise, it would be concordant with scientific laws that life energy remains present despite its no longer being associated with the physical body. The Bhagavad Gita states that the essence of each of us is never destroyed and never dies. Just as a man or woman casts off clothes and puts on new ones,

171

our essence can don new physical representations or take them off. All major religions believe that the soul, the spirit, or the essence of consciousness persists after the physical body is no longer living. Similarly, unique oneness theory holds that consciousness, which harbors our uniqueness, persists despite changes within external reality (our world and universe) and objective internal reality (our physical bodies).

From this perspective, death is in actuality a perceptual illusion. While it is true that physical matter changes form and "dies" in external reality, and that it is perceived accurately within our internal replica of reality, consciousness and life energy aren't perceived as continuing onward. Perhaps this in part is due to the lack of sensory ability to perceive this attribute outside its organic unity with matter. However, it may also be due to the inability to accept this subjective aspect of reality without objective verification. Without a doubt, this life energy remains part of external reality, whether perceived or not. Therefore, the perceived finality of death is simply an illusion. Instead what we perceive as death is simply a transformation no different from a person changing his or her clothes from one day to the next.

Whether consciousness, life energy, or the self reestablishes a new organic entity through processes such as rebirth or reincarnation, it remains a point of philosophical and religious contemplation. This is simply because we are unable to measure, sense, and accurately perceive these nonmaterial phenomena. But just because science has yet to objectively quantify consciousness doesn't mean it should be not included from consideration or theories. To move forward and embrace true reality, science and philosophies within the realm of reality, perception, consciousness, and self must come together. Unique oneness theory is a step in that direction.

Further Philosophical Considerations of Unique Oneness Theory

The Hindu teachings of Sri Ramanuja provided significant influence on the foundations held by unique oneness theory. His philosophies described during his lifetime during the eleventh century remain some of the greatest fundamental philosophies within Eastern cultures and speak to the previously mentioned issues of substance and attributes. His monistic philosophy believed in one God, and he also believed that perceived attributes and qualities in the universe were indeed real, permanent, and under control of this God. This contrasted with Adi Shankara's teachings of his time, which taught that all qualities and attributes of various entities were temporary and outside of true reality.

In considering our example of a red rose again, the redness of a rose, according to Shankara, was a fleeting attribute. Its lack of performance defined its lack of reality. However, Sri Ramanuja felt that attributes were not only real but also inseparable from the object itself. The redness and the rose were organically linked in its presence in reality. Neither could be present independently because both were organically one within the true reality. This occurred because God was ultimately in control of reality and determined how organic connections of qualities and substances existed.

Like Sri Ramanuja, unique oneness theory supports a holistic, true reality that contains integrally related substances and attributes at any given time. These relationships evolve over time, but regardless, one reality is always present, upon which we base our individual perceptions. In this way, everything is linked together within the universe. The examples given within this text concerning recent discoveries in physics (such as the concept of entanglement) support this from an objective standpoint. The universe is continually unraveling before our eyes according to a controlled and possibly predetermined plan. What appears to be chaotic may actually be extremely organized. These findings substantiate the belief that indeed a controlling entity is in charge of external reality throughout all time.

Sri Ramanuja's philosophies also taught that God was integrally related to the world and to all souls or spirits within it. In essence, the world and human souls represented God's body while God's own spirit resided within the world and within all souls throughout the universe. Just as our human bodies cannot exist organically without life energy, the universe (the world and our souls) cannot exist without God. Existence once again depends on the presence of both substance and attribute. When we extrapolate this concept within unique oneness theory, we see that all things exist in reality, including their material substance and characteristics. Additionally, accurate perception of reality requires an ability to recreate a replica of reality that contains all its attributes and material forms. When all attributes aren't considered and recreated, perceived reality falls short of true reality. If this discrepancy is significant, illusions, delusions, and hallucinations occur.

With this in mind, an obvious question arises. How can we enhance our ability to more accurately perceive true reality? How often do we inaccurately perceive a situation based on limited knowledge, limited past experiences, or simply an inability to perceive true form and attribute? People used to believe the earth was flat, given their knowledge and perceptual senses. Was true reality different then, or was our perception of reality flawed due to our own limitations? According to unique oneness theory, the latter is the correct answer. It's likely that what we hold today as valid will indeed prove to be utterly ridiculous in the centuries to come. For us to advance in our abilities to better perceive our universe, we must expand our knowledge while being open to greater subjective possibilities. While the scientific method is wonderful for objective and empirical study, it also handicaps our ability to evolve to a greater perceptual understanding.

Suppose for a moment that we were magically granted a sixth sense, allowing us to now perceive nonmaterial energies. We might be able to see one soul leave a dying body and enter another form of matter. Free energies might be seen intermingling with other energies and other forms to influence outcomes and experiences. It would be like having a pair of infrared goggles to wear at night in a battlefield. Our understanding would be more accurate of true reality simply because we could now objectively sense additional information about our universe. Given the numerous accounts of unexplained occurrences in medical science and beyond, the presence of such immeasurable forces in reality isn't unlikely. It's within the subjective that opportunities for enhanced perceptual abilities exist and where human progress can be made.

Applications of Unique Oneness Theory into the Future

According to the process of perception, as proposed by unique oneness theory, an inseparable, organic unit is created as the brain/mind complex internally generates a nearly precise replica of the external world. Accurate perception depends on this internal system to approximate true reality and optimally function. When considering current applications and future applications of this theory, two main areas are noteworthy. One addresses conditions where the internal system results in false perceptual abilities, and the second considers the ability of the internal system to perceive realities, which are difficult or unable to be currently sensed about our universe.

In some of the latter chapters of this book, medical disorders were discussed that described disruptions of the internal perceptual systems. Visual and auditory hallucinations, thought delusions, visual illusions, and other phenomena resulting from faulty perceptions occur when our brain or mind complex failed to recreate an accurate replica of the true external reality. In some cases, this was due to genetic disturbances, while in others chemical derangements, anatomical changes, or other physiological and psychological derangements accounted for the disturbance. To date, most of the direction of therapy for these conditions has focused only on these underlying causes rather than on adjunctive perceptual aspects.

While the primary etiology of such medical disorders is certainly a key focus, invoking other ancillary therapies that improve perceptual functioning should also be considered. Through psychological therapies, the internal system of perception can be enhanced to more accurately assess external reality. Biofeedback accomplishes this through positive and negative reinforcements in the external environment on the internal perceptual system. Psychotherapy accomplishes this through logic, education, and understanding. Meditation pursues this through enhanced consciousness and the internal subjective aspects of internal perception. In Western cultures, these therapies often take a back seat to medication and surgical therapies. But to provide more comprehensive health care, all these treatments should be used concomitantly.

In addition to therapeutic endeavors, unique oneness theory should also be applied to medical research investigations. The scientific method has dominated medical science for centuries, and without question, its objective format is critical in elucidating accurate results, cause-and-effect relationships, and new directions of study. However, what we currently perceive is only part of true reality, and our ability to expand our knowledge of our universe and our bodies is limited when such a format is used. The development of new research protocols that take the concepts of unique oneness theory into consideration would potentially open new doors for us in the world of medical science. In fact, this ultimately may finally allow a marriage between the worlds of science and philosophy, which has been a long time coming.

The second direction of application is even more intriguing, particularly if you accept that what we are able to perceive through our human senses is only partially complete. This concept isn't necessarily hard to embrace when you realize all the times throughout history when technological advancements allow us to "see" reality from a new and more accurate perspective. Accepting that true reality is composed of aspects that are inaccessible to our internal perceptual system can be difficult. And being trained in a scientific field dependent on concrete objectivity like medicine doesn't facilitate open acceptance of such concepts. However, incredible opportunities to understand universal reality more fully lie beyond what we can actually see, hear, feel, and currently perceive.

When we use the same techniques of biofeedback, logic, and subjective research techniques, we can draw perceptual conclusions from rational evidence of true reality. And since we realize our internal perceptual system can generate its own perceptual images and impressions, perhaps these rational conclusions can be used to assist our internal systems into more accurately portraying reality through internal replicas. If hallucinations, delusions, and illusions can be present in a pathological state, then why can't we generate the same perceptual phenomena that yield super awareness of true reality?

We spoke earlier of death as a potential illusion. The life energy that leaves a physical body cannot be currently perceived by human abilities. But logic supports that this energy is neither created nor destroyed at the time of so-called death. Therefore, death could be perceived differently through invoking new perceptual techniques on our internal perceptual system. New technologies may enable this life energy to be objectively "seen." New research paradigms may enable us to visualize changes that show the flow of this energy from one place to another. The key is that we must be at least receptive to such perceptions that extend beyond our basic human capacities if we are going to take the next step toward greater health and understanding.

While these latter applications of unique oneness theory are more theoretical than the former ones mentioned, they are nonetheless important in advancing medicine, science, and philosophy. Like each of us, these individual branches of study have unique perspectives and perceptions of the world in which we live and of our universe. But also like true reality, each discipline carries within it a significant degree of truth and validity. Each perceives reality from different viewpoints and thus can more accurately define different aspect of reality. By combining the objective and subjective, and by bridging the gap between dualistic perspectives, a more complete and accurate understanding of our universe becomes possible. By combining accurate perceptions from all disciplinary fields, a more complete perception of our universe occurs. This is what unique oneness theory hopes to accomplish by allowing greater understanding of our inner perceptual abilities and by expanding the possibilities available to us in the process. Ultimately, this can lead to greater human potential, improved health and functioning, and a more fulfilling existence in our universe.

Bibliograpy

Chapter 6

1. Edelman, G. M., and J. P. Changeux. The Brain. New York: Transaction Publishers, 2001.

2. Einstein, Albert. *The World as I See It.* Bel Air, CA: Citadel Press, 2001.

3. Thompson, Richard. *God and Science.* Alachua, FL: Goverdhan Hill Publishing, 2004.

4. Thompson, Richard. *Mechanistic and Nonmechanistic Science.* Los Angeles: Bhaktivedanta Book Trust, 1981.

Chapter 7

5. Astin, John A., Elaine Harkness, and Edzard Ernst. "The Efficacy of 'Distant Healing': A Systematic Review of Randomized Trials." Ann Inter Med 132 (June 6, 2000): 903–910.

6. Rubik, Baverly. *Life at the Edge of Science.* Philadelphia, PA: Institute for Frontier Science, 1996.

7. Robert Jahn, "Scientific Study of Consciousness—Related Physical Phenomena," Princeton Engineering Anomalies Research. February 10, 2007,

8. PRINCETON'S PEAR LABORATORY TO CLOSE, http:/ www.princeton.edu/~pear/press_release_closing.html.

9. Mansell, W. "Control Theory and Psychopathology: An Integrative Approach."
   Psychol Psychother 78, Pt 2 (2005): 141–78.

10. Marken, R. S. "Controlled Variables: Psychology as the Center Fielder View It."
    The American Journal of Psychology 114, no. 2 (2001): 259–81.

11. McClelland, Kent. "The Collective Control of Perceptions: Constructing Order from Conflict." *International Journal of Human-Computer Studies* 64, no. 1 (2004): 65–99.

12. Wittmann M, Carter O, Hasler F, Cahn BR, Grimberg U, Spring, P Daniel, Hans Flohr, Franz X. Vollenweider. "Effects of Psilocybin on Time Perception and Temporal Control of Behaviour in Humans." *J Psychopharmacol* 1 (January 21, 2007): 50–64.

13. Beique, J. C., M. Imad, L. Mladenovic, Gingrich JA, Andrade R. "Mechanism of the 5-Hydroxytryptamine 2A Receptor-Medicated Facilitation of Synaptic Activity in Prefrontal Cortex." *Proc Natl Acad Sci U S A* 104 (2007): 9870–5.

14. Gouzoulis-Mayfrank, B. E., Thelen Hermle, H. Sass. "History, Rationale and Potential of Human Experimental Hallucinogenic Drug Research in Psychiatry." *Pharmacopsychiatry* 31 (1998): Suppl 2: 63–8.

15. Aghajanian, G. G. Marek. "Seratonin and Hallucinogens" *Neuropsychopharmacology* 21(S) Sl (1999): 162–23S.

16. Kent, James. (2008). "Selective 5-HT2A Agonist Hallucinogens: A Review of Pharmacological Interaction and Corollary Perceptual Effects."

17. http://www.tripzine.com/pit/html/multi-state-theory.htm.

Printed in the United States
By Bookmasters